PHENOMENOLOGY
AND LOGIC

PHENOMENOLOGY AND LOGIC

Robert S. Tragesser

CORNELL UNIVERSITY PRESS

ITHACA AND LONDON

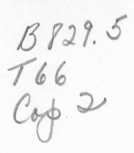

First published 1977 by Cornell University Press.
Published in the United Kingdom by Cornell University Press Ltd.,
2–4 Brook Street, London W1Y 1AA.

International Standard Book Number 0–8014–1068–1
Library of Congress Catalog Card Number 76–28025
Printed in the United States of America by Vail-Ballou Press, Inc.
Librarians: Library of Congress cataloging information
appears on the last page of the book.

TO SUSAN

Contents

| Preface

David Hilbert, in the late nineteenth century, solved a fa-
mous open problem in algebra by using what at the time
seemed to be deviant logical principles,[1] and this method
exposed a great but little-acknowledged problem in the foundations of logic: how can we give a full justification for a
choice among logical principles for the purposes of formulating scientific theories of considered objective domains,
considered worlds? The extent to which logical principles
are exhausted by their formal content is arguable, and thus
so is the extent to which *informal* analysis can and must guide
and establish *formal* analysis. It is the purpose of this book to
show that there are in fact *informal,* nonempirical considerations that enable us to decide among logics, and that these
considerations offer the possibility of producing reasons for
making such choices superior to the positivistic criteria of
fruitfulness and simplicity. The considerations presented
here are phenomenological in character.

The following pages offer an introduction to what might
be thought of as *naive* phenomenology or, what is the same
thing, phenomenological psychology.[2] The latter is concerned
with the philosophic consequences of fully examining and

1. See Constance Reid, *Hilbert* (New York, 1970), Chapter 5.
2. Edmund Husserl, *Ideas* (New York, 1969), especially "Author's
Preface to the English Edition."

describing the formations of experience that come into view when one shifts from the natural direction of experience, which is toward objects, and reflects on the stream of experience, of consciousness. Clearly distinguishing phenomenological psychology from transcendental phenomenology is a profound problem. The latter not only shares the concerns of the former, but in addition aims to give a theoretical foundation to the findings of phenomenological psychology, in adequately ascertaining accessible laws governing the "constitution" of what is found under phenomenological reflection. To use the jargon of the subject—transcendental phenomenology is concerned to produce through phenomenological reflection the "constitutive Apriori" of all domains of being, the essential laws governing the experience or consciousness of anything whatsoever.

The main difficulty with formulating a transcendental phenomenology is that, since Husserl, it seems necessary to introduce theoretical entities which are intensional in character. In the current state of our understanding of intensional entities (e.g., meanings, concepts), their introduction creates many more problems than it effectively solves. Transcendental phenomenology, however, flows from phenomenological psychology, and it is possible to achieve some insights proper to transcendental phenomenology without fully committing oneself to Husserl's theory of noematic *Sinne*. These insights have some value even though their fully adequate formulation will require a theoretical commitment at least as strong as Husserl's commitment in his theory. What I have written stands in the misty border region between phenomenological psychology and a full transcendental phenomenology. My feeling is that by retreating to a naive phenomenology and from that perspective pushing afresh toward transcendental phenomenology I stand a better chance of seeing how to develop a transcendental phenomenology. I make no claim to explain or interpret Husserl's philosophy. What I hope to show is that by taking the phenomenological viewpoint seriously one is led to insights into the foundations of logic.

This book addresses several problems in the foundations of logic, showing that phenomenological work may very well help to solve them, and how:

1. Where do we find reasons better than arbitrary for choosing among alternative logics for the purpose of formulating scientific theories of considered objective domains, worlds? (Proposed answer: phenomenological reflection.)

2. Is logic empirical or nonempirical (transcendental)? (Proposed answer: Chapter IV gives us reason to believe that it is nonempirical, but not "analytic.")

3. Can there be a cognitively contentual criterion for the existence of worlds? (Chapter III provides such a criterion.)

4. Is there a sense in which we may rightly be said to observe abstract entities? (Proposed answer: yes, as shown in Chapter I.)

5. What in our intellectual experience fixes a world as a constant object of scientific study? (Is there something in our intellectual experience that provides for a rigid designation of worlds?) (Proposed answer: yes, viz., $Val(p,t,i)$ as discussed in Chapter III and the Appendix.)

Various other topics arise, among them the problem of mind-independent truth-bearers, the problem of finding reasons for choosing classical logic, and the problem of the adequacy of Alfred Tarski's explanation of "truth" raised by the existence of several concepts of "truth."

The main results found in Chapter IV may be regarded as foundational insights justifying not any particular theorem that can be formulated with rigor, but rather the adoption of a certain philosophical perspective on the relevance of formal developments in logic for the understanding of rational experience. I try to make clear how the phenomenological content of rational experience directed toward a certain world regulates the choice of logic for that world, how it in a sense enables us to "lift the logic off the world."

A central task of philosophy is to give a full account of the contents of intellectual experience, perhaps the most profound of which are the so-called "experiences of truth," such as proof, demonstration, and intuitive "self-evidence." There are two ways of approaching a theory of the contents of intellectual experience—the phenomenological and the reductive. The phenomenological method essentially elaborates the contents of intellectual experience on their own grounds. For example, I am presented with a proof or a species of proof and I attempt, by unpacking it through reflective scrutiny, to characterize and understand all its elements as they display themselves and, more or less solely on this ground, to determine its cognitive worth and the limits of its validity. The reductive method attempts to explain or codify and evaluate the contents of intellectual experience "from the outside." Here we find the great metaphysical systems as well as the psychologistic, physicalistic, and linguistic or logical reductive enterprises.

Every successful reductive enterprise that genuinely "reduces" a content of intellectual experience must be founded on some phenomenological work, for otherwise there could be no guarantee that the "reduction" indeed applied to the purported object being reduced, for example, that certain logical laws can be adequately reduced to, or treated as, psychological laws. One effective way of criticizing, for example, Hume's reduction of concepts is to return to our intellectual experience of how concepts appear and function and see if Hume's quasi-psychologistic reduction genuinely accounts for all aspects of the concepts as they manifest themselves under reflective, phenomenological, scrutiny.

Reductive efforts are unquestionably highly instructive, if

only because their typical brashness sometimes throws into relief unnoticed aspects of the purportedly reduced entities, thus serving to warn us that our phenomenology has not been thorough enough. But a question arises as to how much philosophic progress can be made on the foundation of phenomenological reflection with a minimum of psychologistic, metaphysical, physicalistic, behavioristic, linguistic, or logical reduction. It is one of my tasks to clarify the phenomenological point of view and to show that it has a nontrivial bearing on a philosophic problem. The problem I have chosen is, as I have said, how to determine reasons better than arbitrary for choosing one logic over another for the purposes of formulating scientific theories of a considered world, a considered objective domain.

I have not assumed that the reader has studied phenomenology. For those interested in an introduction to the subject, a clear interpretation of Husserl's transcendental phenomenological theory in the spirit of the Fregean so-called "Stanford school of phenomenology"—an interpretation I have found very helpful in gaining phenomenological insight from Husserl—is to be found in the papers of Dagfinn Føllesdal, as well as those by David Smith and Ronald MacIntyre, listed in the Bibliography. (For an interesting anti-Fregean interpretation of Husserl, see Hubert Dreyfus' study of Husserl's concept of noemata, also listed in the Bibliography.) Gian-Carlo Rota's short but highly suggestive article is of value for its striking picture of the way in which phenomenological thinking underlies scientific thinking, especially with reference to mathematics and physics.

I gratefully acknowledge the sometimes considerable intellectual and moral support of James Street Fulton, Richard J. Hall, Kathryn Pyne Parsons, W. W. Tait, and Jeffrey Ian Zucker. Zucker has faithfully read and commented on all previous versions of this work. Dagfinn Føllesdal read the penultimate version and made several helpful suggestions. My wife, Susan, has proposed changes that helped to clarify the text. Discussions with Dagfinn Føllesdal, Hubert Dreyfus, John Hoagueland, and others during a summer-long seminar at Stanford in 1975 impressed upon me the importance of keeping phenomenological psychology as distinct as possible from transcendental phenomenology.

ROBERT S. TRAGESSER

Kenosha, Wisconsin

PHENOMENOLOGY
AND LOGIC

| Introduction

Phenomenological considerations promise to yield the best understanding of Kurt Gödel's mathematical Platonism, and it seems that a least eristic path to an appreciation of phenomenology is to point out how phenomenology can yield such an understanding. I will follow such a path, making Gödel's study "What Is Cantor's Continuum Problem?" the focus of concern.

It happens frequently in our intellectual and perceptual experience that we are given or presented with an object, we have an intellectual or perceptual "grasp" on the object, but our "grasp" is incomplete, and we know this. For example, I see a tree and know that there are many aspects of it (e.g., fungi on the bark, the other side of the tree, the roots) which now I either cannot see or cannot see perfectly. Or, I am presented with an argument supporting a thesis, and I am aware that I do not fully understand how it hangs together, that there are aspects I must attend to if I am adequately to decide its validity.

The term 'prehension' will be used for such an imperfect or incomplete "grasp" of a purportedly objective state of affairs, where it is somehow known that the state of affairs is imperfectly or incompletely given. Otherwise stated—a *prehension* is an inadequate or imperfect grasp of something, where the content of the grasp adumbrates or points to something beyond what is given. Prehension is a form of incomplete cognitive apprehension.

To see the point of taking into account the adumbration of more than is fully given, consider the examples of the prehension of the tree and that of the argument. In both cases, the prehension contains *Leitfaden,* hints of paths, where following them will lead to a more complete apprehension of the considered object. The very elements of one's "grasp," one's prehension, point the way to a more complete apprehension of the considered object. I see, for example, that I inadequately observe the fungi on the bark and that walking and looking more closely will enable me to see it better. Or, I see that I am not sure about the significance of a step in the considered argument, but that by attending more closely to the argument's relevant phases in such and such ways I can determine the significance of the step.

A prehension frames or fixes its object; on the foundations of the elements of the prehension, I can find my way to a more complete apprehension of the object, for the elements lead to or adumbrate further aspects of the object. The pursuit of what is adumbrated in the prehension, as we smoothly, continuously, disperse the shadows, not only leads to a more complete apprehension. Also, and most importantly, because of the harmony or continuity between the phases of our increasingly improved apprehension, as the front of the tree foreshadows the back or as the presentation of a succession of statements leads to a perception of the logical relations among them, this kind of cognitive pursuit provides us with the insight and rational conviction that we are indeed achieving a more complete apprehension of *the same thing.* The harmonious or compatible seemingly continuous phases in the growth of apprehension, phases adumbrated in antecedent prehensions, provide a clear picture of the self-identity of the object of concern through the growth of apprehension. One can not help but see that *this* is a further aspect of *that*.

Prehension is fallible. It may construe *this* object as a tree or *this* object as a sensible argument. Under this construal a barked other side is adumbrated by at least the apparent curvature of the trunk of the prehended tree; or fully sensible, validly connected, phases of an argument are adumbrated by the seemingly sensible way in which the superficially viewed argument hangs together. It may happen, however, that following out the paths of observation and consideration suggested by the adumbrations produces quite conflicting observations: looking at the other side of "the tree" shows me a cardboard back, or attending more closely to the sentences in the considered argument reveals cleverly concealed nonsense. When, in fact, we *cannot* achieve an increasingly perfect apprehension of a prehended object, when adumbrations prove to be false leads, we may find ourselves ready to suggest that the object as prehended, as initially taken or grasped, does *not* exist. As long as increasingly perfect apprehension is possible and continues, however, I think that we are currently justified in saying that what we are prehending exists, that it has some kind of objective being.

With these easy phenomenological insights into the "contents" of prehensions before us, we are in a position to discuss Gödel's mathematical Platonism. The phenomenological insights will be deepened, extended, and made somewhat more precise in later chapters, thus making possible a complete accounting of Gödel's Platonism. The central aim of the present work, however, is to motivate a search for deeper and more complete phenomenological insights, at least on the grounds that they would illuminate Gödel's Platonism, related ontological attitudes, and the foundations of logic.

Cantor's continuum problem is the question: How many

different sets of integers exist? [1] Cantor's continuum hypothesis (abbreviated CH) is that the answer is the second infinite cardinal number. Paul Cohen proved that, given the consistency of von Neumann-Bernays axioms of set theory (the axiom of choice included), then these axioms plus CH and these axioms plus not-CH both form consistent systems; that is, the truth or falsity of CH is not decided by the axioms.[2] In fact, no compelling axioms have been discovered which decided CH. The questions is: Is CH true or false? This question clearly assumes a well-determined reality, a well-determined objective domain, deciding all sentences expressible in the language of set theory. What right do we have to assert the existence of such a domain, and thus what right do we have to assert that CH is either true or false, and true or false independently of our knowledge of its truth or falsity?

Gödel argues that we have the right to assert the existence of such a well-determined reality. His arguments can be refined by phenomenological considerations so that certain more or less fine points made in his study are given their due. These points will be developed in a broad context in Chapters I and III, but it seems worthwhile to consider them now in the very specific context of Gödel's essay. We have already made the pertinent phenomenological observations above.

On what grounds are we justified in asserting the existence of *the* domain of set theory S as a well-determined reality in which, say, CH is true or false? The principal grounds are that S is prehended and, on the foundation of this prehension, one can find many paths promising more complete apprehensions of S possibly decisive for CH. Just as in walking around a prehended tree our expectations inspired by adum-

1. Kurt Gödel, "What Is Cantor's Continuum Problem?" in *Philosophy of Mathematics,* ed. P. Benacerraf and H. Putnam (Englewood Cliffs, N.J., 1964), p. 258.

2. Paul J. Cohen, *Set Theory and the Continuum Hypothesis* (Menlo Park, Calif., 1966).

brations in our prehension may be exploded, so following the paths promising a more complete apprehension of S may lead to a collapse of sense, hopeless conceptual confusions, and other such aporias. But, as I will explain in more detail in Chapter III, in the absence of such aporias, and in the presence of promising, increasingly complete apprehension of S, it is difficult to deny the existence of S—one's actual intellectual experience preserves one's sense of what is prehended, viz., S, as a well-determined reality having a life of its own independent of one's will and desire. This is essentially Gödel's point, as I will now show.

First, Gödel argues that we have a strong prehension of the domain of set theory S where the objects in S, viz., sets, are taken as "something obtainable from the integers (or some other well-defined objects) by iterated application of the operation 'set of', not something obtained by dividing the totality of all existing things into two categories." He then claims that this prehension of S "has never led to any antinomy whatsoever; that is, the perfectly 'naive' and uncritical working with this concept of set has so far proved completely self-consistent." He explains that in our present state of knowledge, "the operation 'set of x's' (where x ranges over some given kind of objects) can not be defined satisfactorily." [3] Our understanding of the operation, however, our prehension of it, seems to have enough integrity to yield much solid mathematical theory encoded in axiomatic set theory. (The reader is referred to the articles by Black and Stenius in the Bibliography for a critique of the notions *set* and *set of*.)

Second, as Gödel writes:

It is to be noted, however, that on the basis of the point of view here adopted, a proof of the undecidability of Cantor's conjecture from the accepted axioms of set theory . . . would by no

3. Gödel, "What Is Cantor's Continuum Problem?" pp. 262–263.

means solve the problem. For if the meanings of the primitive terms of set theory are as explained [in the passages referred to above], it follows that the set-theoretical concepts and theorems describe some well-determined reality, in which Cantor's conjecture must either be true or false. Hence its undecidability from the axioms being assumed today can only mean that these axioms do not contain a complete description of that reality. Such a belief is by no means chimerical, since it is possible to point out ways in which the decision of a question, which is undecidable from the usual axioms, might nevertheless be obtained.[4]

The extremely crucial statement here is the last: "Such a belief is by no means chimerical, since it is possible to point out ways in which the decision of a question, which is undecidable from the usual axioms, might nevertheless be obtained." What is so important in this statement is the tie it makes between our right to say that S is a well-determined reality (in which, say, CH is decided) and the discoverability of promising ways in which open problems (e.g., CH) about the domain could be decided. Gödel spends the remainder of the article presenting possible paths to a decision about CH. As long as we can find such paths, S will seem the well-determined reality we initially took it to be.

Of course, no small part of our continued conviction in the well-determinateness of S is the fact that we can insightfully and compellingly see that *if* such and such a path were followed leading to a consideration seemingly deciding CH, *then* we are within our rights to call CH decided. That is, no small part of our continued conviction in the well-determinateness of S is the fact that we can come up with ways of deciding CH, or ways that promise to decide CH, which do not lead to an institution of the truth or falsity of CH by convention, by fiat, by arbitrary choice. We insightfully see that such and such considerations are indeed con-

4. Ibid., pp. 263–264.

siderations aimed at the same, self-identical prehended objectivity S.

Where do the ideas for such nonarbitrary, fully legitimated paths of consideration come from? What gives us the assurance that if following these paths produced insights, then these insights could rightfully and without fiat or arbitrariness be construed as yielding a better apprehension of the same domain S? The answer is basically the same as in the cases of our examples of the perceptual prehension of a tree and the prehension of an argument: adumbrations of further aspects when followed out produce a continuity of phases of observation and consideration preserving the identity of the prehended object. For example, in one instance in which Gödel is determining where new axioms might come from, he says, "First of all the axioms of set theory by no means form a system closed in itself, but, quite on the contrary, the very concept of set [= concept of sets = the initial prehension of S described above] on which they are based suggests their extension by new axioms which assert the existence of still further iterations of the operation 'set of'. These axioms can be formulated also as propositions asserting the existence of very great cardinal numbers." [5] That is, the elements of the prehension of S, like the elements of my prehension of a tree, lead immediately to a path of consideration leading to further aspects of the prehended object, aspects having the character of being adumbrated in the prehension, e.g., the possibility of continuing the operation "set of," thus bringing more of S into view.

Gödel may be viewed as giving an analysis of the elements of the prehension of S and, on the foundation of that analysis, showing how CH could possibly be decided. Such analysis, because it reflects faithfully upon, and describes, the elements of an act of consciousness (a prehension, in this case), is

5. Ibid., p. 264.

phenomenological analysis. We can see here the critical importance of such analysis, viz., that it provides possible paths to reasons rather better than arbitrary for holding something to be true of a considered object or objective domain. For this reason, phenomenological analysis is not without foundational significance for all of the sciences. A foundational scheme for *Wissenschaften* like physics or logic, biology or geology, mathematics or theology, is successful to the extent that it maximizes our intellectual or rational control over them, and to the extent that it maximizes our ability to eliminate arbitrariness or conventionality in emergent theories, to replace dogma by understanding, guesses and beliefs by reasons, cloudiness by clarity, and fever by thought. In the sense that Gödel's phenomenological analysis provides the hope of reasons better than arbitrary and, in fact, perfectly sound mathematical reasons, for accepting or rejecting CH, phenomenology has a contribution to make to the foundation of the sciences.

We will briefly return to the example from Gödel later (in Chapter III in particular) when we have had a chance to work out in more detail some of the considerations presented above, especially those purportedly justifying us in asserting the existence of S as a well-determined reality. The purpose of this book, however, is *not* to give a full foundation to Gödel's mathematical Platonism or even fully to exploit the ontological insights implicit in the phenomenological construal of Gödel's studies. Rather, I have taken a problem which seems to me to be crucial for the future of scientific thought and for logic in particular. We have seen that the phenomenological analysis, the analysis of the "content" of conscious acts, promises to provide compelling reasons better than arbitrary for holding something to be true of a considered object and so of showing us how, rightly and justifiably, to improve our apprehension of an objectivity or objectuality. The results can be quite nontrivial; e.g., one should keep in mind not only Gödel's article, but also the not farfetched remark of Gian-Carlo Rota that, to use my phrasing, a closer (phenomenological) analysis of the elements of the prehension of (physical) simultaneity than had ever been attempted before led Einstein to crucial aspects of his relativity theory.[6]

The question I am asking in this work is this: Can phenomenological analysis provide us with reasons better than arbitrary for choosing among possible logics for the purposes of constructing and formulating adequate, true, scientific theories of considered objective domains, worlds? I see phenomenological work as yielding instructive answers to this question, a question of importance to us in view of the coherent formal and semantic development of various alternatives to classical logic. I am interested in making some progress toward answering the question asked by Hao Wang and W. V. Quine: "How much better than arbitrary is our particular quantification theory [classical, objectual quantification theory], seen as one in a possible spectrum of quantification theory?"[7] It will be the task of Chapter IV to approach one part of this problem in a way that fruitfully complicates the problem. I will argue on phenomenological grounds that there exist objective domains, worlds, requiring nonclassical logic. The existence of sound, interpreted alternative logics and the existence of worlds requiring them for the purposes of formulating scientific theories of those worlds make it difficult for any rational person to use classical, objectual logic uncritically. We are thereby forced to find reasons better than arbitrary for using classical logic. Ironically,

6. "Edmund Husserl and the Reform of Logic," in *Explorations in Phenomenology*, ed. D. Carr and E. S. Casey (The Hague, 1973), pp. 299–305 and p. 305 in particular.

7. W. V. Quine, *Ontological Relativity and Other Essays* (New York, 1969), p. 108.

it is classical logic that is, I think, most difficult to justify. It is promising that phenomenological brooding provides us with reasons better than arbitrary for sometimes choosing classical logic. These reasons turn out to be "transcendental" and thus nonempirical, and certainly of a nature remote from considerations of "fruitfulness and simplicity" (construed, of course, in a way yielding, between fruitfulness and fruitlessness, simplicity and complexity, distinctions well marked by differences).

The attentive reader will already have noticed a hint of the connection between phenomenological analysis and the possibility of deciding among logics: this hint emerged when it was pointed out how phenomenological considerations lead us to be justified in asserting the existence of S as a well-determined reality, a reality in which CH is either true or false, a reality, in particular, where the law of the excluded middle (and bivalence, if one cares to make a distinction) is justified (all sentences in the language of set theory are true or false). It is the purpose of what follows to strengthen such considerations.

I | The Observation of Abstract Entities

A principal application of phenomenology is described as follows. One begins with an experience (either intellectual or sensual) wherein one's attention certainly seems to be directed toward an entity of such and such a kind and that entity seems to be presented sufficiently for one to be warranted in making sound assertions about it. Possible examples of such objects are: physical things, numbers, high-energy particles, values, the nature of dimension, prices, stars, temperatures, ordered pairs, the physical nature of simultaneity, the meaning of 'Russell believed that round squares exist'. Beginning with reflection on the apparent presentative experience of such an entity, the phenomenologist looks very closely at the experience to determine whether or not, on the ground of such an experience, whether intellectual or sensual, one has any right to treat the entity as it appeared at first glance, as existing and as accessible to justifiable assertion.

The task of I.1 is to cultivate by phenomenological reflection a criterion determining when we are justified in asserting the existence of purported abstract objects. As the reader of Husserl's *Ideas* (or of Føllesdal's writings on Husserl) is aware, Husserl purports to discover by phenomenological reflection that our experience of an external world is made possible by certain intensional entities called 'noemata'. Frege purports to make a similar discovery, which will be discussed in I.2. The reader must take care to understand my attitude toward I.2. I wish to take a neutral attitude toward the existence of intensional entities in the sense that I will avoid, as much as I can, doing phenomenology which assumes them. Thus, I will not enter fully into the domain of Husserlian transcendental phenomenology. In I.1, I.2, and I.3, however, I say as much as I can on behalf of their existence. In particular, in I.3 I try to disentangle the problem of accepting intensional entities as existing from the problem of linguistic meaning, in this small measure freeing us to take seriously Husserlian claims about the existence of noemata, "meanings." The problem is to learn to apply the criterion for the existence of abstract entities to this particular case. I would not have made so much of this matter if I thought learning this impossible. The principal applications I shall make of the criterion of I.1, however, are (1) to argue that phenomena—to be introduced in II—are objectual, that they exist and are legitimate objects of study, and (2) to apply the criterion analogically to the question of determining the existence of purported worlds, objective domains.

Although I am trying to refrain from doing Husserlian transcendental phenomenology, in doing phenomenological psychology I must nevertheless take account of what seems to be intensional entities which do indeed have certain analogies with Husserlian "noemata"; these are the "conceptions," "$Val(p,t,i)$'s," etc., discussed in Chapter III and the Appendix. These seemingly intensional entities just seem to be there in the phenomenological field. I am reporting what I find there. I refrain, however, from claiming the last word on their nature. By the criterion of "objective existence" developed here, they seem "objectively existent." Unlike Husserl of the *Ideas,* I think, I prefer to allow that what might seem like intensional entities at a phenomenological level might turn out not to be such entities. I refrain from attempting a theoretical explanation of such entities while still acknowledging their *presence to mind.*

I.1. The Analogy with Perception

First, a historical example.

The Pythagoreans proved that there are incommensurable magnitudes. This left them with no idea of how to think about arbitrary magnitudes. They did not need an adequate theory of the identity and existence of magnitudes to be compelled to admit that incommensurable magnitudes in particular exist. Eudoxus' theory of magnitudes [1] and the rather Eudoxian characterization of the real numbers by Richard Dedekind [2] together show that the real numbers are adequate for quantitizing all possible "Archimedian" magnitudes. Even so, there are still large gaps in our knowledge of the real numbers. We do not know how many there are. This suggests a fundamental failure to grasp their "principle of individuation." That is, after over two thousand years, in this comparatively ideal context (mathematics), we still do not have a fully satisfactory theory of magnitudes. But failure of satisfaction of this sort is not grounds for denying the existence of, say, the square root of two; such grounds were not sufficient even at the beginning for denying its existence. Together with its property of "irrationality," it stood too clearly before the mind, even if one had no idea of how to understand it more fully.

1. Euclid, *Euclid's Elements,* ed. and trans. T. L. Heath (New York, 1956), book 5.
2. "Continuity and Irrational Numbers," in *Theory of Numbers* (New York, 1963).

The example has a moral. It is that our thought may compellingly present us with an entity or seeming entity which we are poorly prepared to grasp theoretically (e.g., we can not give satisfactorily rational criteria determining its existence and identity), but if such an entity, *just as it appears,* has properties compellingly and insightfully ascribed to it, and if it plays a role of importance in our intellectual experience, then we would be ill-advised to renounce it just because it is poorly understood. One must also be very careful about trying to fill its role with a less problematic entity or construction, for the original entity may have a deeper, but still obscure, role to play.

I will use the term 'abstract entity' not only for, e.g., mathematical objects, properties, values, but also for intensional entities, if such there be, such as meanings, concepts, ideas.

Reflecting straightforwardly on our intellectual experience, at this simplest phenomenological level of consideration I think that we must say that we in some strong sense *observe* abstract entities. More exactly, we *prehend* them (see the Introduction) and, on the foundation of that prehension, can typically achieve further, more complete, apprehension of them, apprehension having the character of being "objective," nonarbitrary, independent of our will and desire. I will now give some further examples of "prehension." Both perceptual experience and the intellective grasp of abstract objects are modes of "observation," of cognitive apprehension. The insight that I will try to cultivate in the following pages is that, *thanks to prehension, abstract objects are just as "real" as, say, the objects of sense perception, as physical things.* The two most important properties that give a prehended object such a strong characteristic of "being real" are these: (1) I am aware at least upon reflection on the conscious act, the prehension, that here is something—what is prehended—that I can not arbitrarily ascribe properties to, here is something having a life independent of my whims, and (2) I can find clear and compelling considerations which can, without arbitrariness and with vindicating, justifying, insight, yield a further, more complete, apprehension of the prehended entity.

Example 1. Remembering can yield a prehension of the remembered. Suppose that I "remember" a person in such a way that I cannot give, on the basis of my memory, a description that would enable someone else to pick him out, but I am aware that I could identify him if I saw him; I could pick him out of a crowd. My memory provides a weak prehension of the remembered; and although my memory is dim, ways occur to me in which I could improve my apprehension of the remembered, e.g., by studying faces, seeking out concrete images of familiar elements identifying the prehended, the remembered. That is, I am aware of more given in my memory than is adequately given. My memory is adumbrating or pointing to specific facial features which are not themselves adequately given, but are given sufficiently so that by proceeding in the suggested manner I could achieve an adequate grasp of those features, when bright, clear, actually perceived features come into perceptible or noticeable harmony or coincidence with the dimly remembered features.

Example 2. In his book *Symmetry*, Hermann Weyl shows by convincing stages how one progresses from prehensions of symmetry in perceptual things to a compelling analysis of all possible spatial symmetries in terms of algebraic structures called 'groups of transformations' (i.e., sets of space-transforming 1:1 onto functions preserving the rigidity of space and satisfying under function composition the properties of an algebraic group). Weyl begins with an analysis of "bilateral symmetry, the symmetry of left and right, which is so conspicuous in the structure of higher animals, especially the human body." He analyzes such elementary symmetries in terms of transformations of space and proceeds by easy stages to the analysis of increasingly complex symmetries, e.g., ornamental and space-filling symmetries:

First I will discuss bilateral symmetry in some detail and its role in art as well as organic and inorganic nature. Then we shall generalize this concept gradually, in the direction indicated by our example of rotational symmetry, first staying within the confines of geometry, but then going beyond these limits through the process of mathematical abstraction along a road that will finally lead us to a mathematical idea of great generality, the Platonic idea as it were behind the special appearance of symmetry.[3]

Thus Weyl moves by easy but compelling and mutually harmonious stages of apprehension, from prehensions of special appearances as appearances of "symmetry" to an increasingly full apprehension of the nature of symmetry. Reading Weyl's pages one has the strong sensation that the stages of his analysis are made not arbitrarily, but on the foundation of increasingly clear and more compelling insights into the nature of symmetry, a nature which showed only vaguely at the beginning.

To certain degrees this scheme is typical for all theoretical knowledge: We begin with some vague principle, . . . then find an important case where we can give that notion a concrete precise meaning (bilateral symmetry), and from that case we gradually rise again to generality, guided more by mathematical construction and abstraction than by the mirages of philosophy; and if we are lucky we end up with an idea no less universal than the one from which we started. Gone may be much of its emotional appeal, but it has the same or even greater unifying power in the realm of thought and is exact instead of vague.[4]

A unity, a nature, a structure, an "idea," vaguely adumbrated in initial clear prehensions of symmetric objects, emerges

3. Hermann Weyl, *Symmetry* (Princeton, N.J., 1952), pp. 2–3.
4. Ibid., p. 3.

as something increasingly apprehended as those prehensions and the mathematical analysis of their contents lead with seeming inexorability to the mathematical idea of symmetry. As each phase of analysis leads harmoniously and compellingly to the next, there is a strong awareness that what one must say is out of one's hands, not a matter of one's will or desire; there is no free choice. In short, one has the strong impression of "observing" something objectual, precisely as, in the case of his search for new axioms for set theory (as discussed briefly in the Introduction), Gödel was guided by adumbrations of further aspects of the universe of set theory, adumbrations contained in the initial prehension.

These examples, and countless others like them deriving from intellectual experience, certainly *suggest* that abstract entities are not illusions, that they are object-like, objectual. I think that this apparent objectivity must have been what impressed Plato so deeply. In any case, if one does not bring any preformed metaphysical disposition or reductionist compulsions to bear on the matter, if one takes intellectual experience as it is (successfully!) lived, at face value, *phenomenologically,* then I think one is compelled by such examples to grant that there is some sense in which we observe abstract entities, if only because in fact we seem to be able to direct our attention and thought to them and, most importantly, we find our thoughts so directed constrained (I find that I can not think anything I want to about the considered entity) and enriched (not with *blind compulsions* to say this or that, but with a genuine *sense of insight*—an important distinction made by Franz Brentano in *The True and the Evident*).

In the remainder of this section I will attempt to make precise the analogy between perceptual observation and the observation of abstract entities, showing as plainly as possible the terms or features on which they agree. Typically, two errors stand in the way of fully appreciating this analogy. The first error is to insist on imposing the categories of a faculty psychology and requiring proof of the existence of a faculty which makes possible observation of abstract entities. What is important and deserves priority is the phenomenological fact of the observation of such entities. If a faculty psychology can explain this, so much the better; if not, should we not doubt the veracity of the faculty phychology rather than disregard the compelling character of our observations? What right does a particular faculty psychology have to steal from us the presented objects, the observed abstract objects, because it fails to find a clearly definable faculty behind the presentation? In any case, Hanson in *Pattern of Discovery* has shown how even ordinary perception involves a great confusing of "faculties." [5]

The second error is physicalism and other such reductionist enterprises. Physicalism gives first priority to the perception of the physical world. But what gives us the right to give such priority to the *Evidenz* of perception over and against other equally compelling forms of *Evidenz?* To make a Husserlian point,[6] one must always begin with some form of *Evidenz;* but each carries with it the limits of its own validity and its correlated objectualities. We may have no interest in considering certain sorts of objectualities or we may be able to fill their role with other objectualities, but this does not deny them their "reality" and does not deny the validity of the correlated *Evidenz.* Simply because we can do without them, we have no right to deny their reality. Logical reduction may allow parsimony in what we take seriously, but it can not deny that there might be something to the objectivity we have cleverly avoided committing ourselves to.

5. N. R. Hanson, *Patterns of Discovery* (Cambridge, 1969).

6. Edmund Husserl, *The Idea of Phenomenology,* trans. W. P. Alston and G. Nakhnikian (The Hague, 1964); and *Cartesian Meditations,* trans. D. Cairns (The Hague, 1960), First Meditation.

Plato, of course, believed and Neo-Platonists, up through Frege, Alonzo Church, and Kurt Gödel, have convinced themselves that there is a sense in which we perceive abstract objects. One finds some Neo-Platonists speaking of "the eye of the soul," "the mind's vision," and the like.[7] These efforts at analogy were prompted not by vague hopes, but by the actual phenomenological content of perceptual and intellectual experience. It is not easy to make a perfect analogy between sense-perception and the purported kind of observation or perception underlying our insight into, or understanding of, abstract entities. There seems to be nothing in our observation of abstract entities corresponding to the sensory or hyletic dimension of sense-perception. I think, however, that the following partial analogy can convince us that abstract objects are just as deservingly thought of as objects, and as *observable* objects, as sense-perceptual objects.

Sense-perceived objects are objectual in that we seem to be able to direct our thoughts to them and find our thoughts constrained and pulled in certain directions by them. Once we undertake a description of a sense-perceived object, there is a certain inevitability about the outcome. The resulting description of the sense-perceived object will compellingly seem to express a correct, insightful characterization of that object.	Abstract entities are objectual in that we seem to be able to direct our thoughts to them and find our thoughts constrained and pulled in certain directions by them. Once we undertake a description of an abstract object, there is a certain inevitability about the outcome. The resulting description of the abstract entity will compellingly seem to express a correct insightful characterization of the entity.

7. Paul Friedländer, *Plato* (New York, 1958), pp. 13–14.

In recent times several philosophers have found such considerations convincing; they have maintained that we observe
abstract objects and, therefore, that they exist. Frege: "Sense-
perception indeed is often thought to be the most certain,
even to be the sole, source of knowledge about everything
that does not belong to the inner world. But with what
right?" Church: "To those who object to the introduction of
abstract entities at all I would say that there are more important criteria by which a theory should be judged. The ex-
treme demand for a simple prohibition of abstract entities
under all circumstances perhaps arises from the desire to
maintain the connection between theory and observation.
But the preference of (say) *seeing* over *understanding* as a
method of observation seems to me capricious. For just as an
opaque body may be seen, so a concept may be understood
or grasped." And Gian-Carlo Rota: "Physical objects (such
as chairs, tables, stars, and so forth) have the same 'degree' of
reality as ideal objects (such as prices, poems, values, emo-
tions, Riemann surfaces, subatomic particles, and so forth).
Nevertheless, the naive prejudice that physical objects are
somehow more 'real' than ideal objects remains one of the
most deeply rooted of Western culture . . . (most of Husserl's critique of Hume pivots around this one issue [see Husserl's *Logical Investigations,* Investigation III])." [8]

In reference to examples similar to those I have given
above (Weyl and Gödel), Husserl remarks that

Inspection of each instance will . . . yield the conviction that
a Species [intensional entity] really becomes an object of knowledge, and that judgments of the same logical force are possible in

8. G. Frege, "The Thought," in *Philosophical Logic,* ed. P. F. Strawson (Oxford, 1968), p. 29; Alonzo Church, "The Need for Abstract Entities in Semantics," in *The Structure of Language,* ed. J. W. Fodor
and J. J. Katz (Englewood Cliffs, N.J., 1964), p. 442; Gian-Carlo Rota,
"Edmund Husserl and the Reform of Logic," in *Explorations in Phenomenology,* ed. D. Carr and E. S. Casey (The Hague, 1973), p. 301.

relation to it, as is the case with individual objects . . . [in reference to] this very idea [of] *the theorem of Pythagorous.* . . . We . . . would point out that each such meaning certainly counts as a unit in our thought and that on occasion we pass evident judgements upon it as a unit: it can be compared with other meanings and distinguished from them. . . . As self-identical, it can in its turn serve as the object of many new meanings. All these things are the same in its case as in the case of other objects, e.g., horses, stones, mental acts . . . that are not meanings. A meaning can be treated as self-identical only because it is self-identical. This argument we find unassailable: it applies to all specific unities [= abstract objects], even to such as are not meanings.[9]

I can sum up the attitude toward abstract objects cultivated here by presenting a criterion for justifiably (which is *not* to say *infallibly*) asserting the existence of an apparent abstract object. This criterion is suggested by the analogy with perception and the quotations from Husserl and others given above.

Criterion for the Justified Assertability of the Existence of Purported Entities. We certainly seem to be able to direct our thoughts toward abstract objects, and we seem, typically, to find our thoughts so directed constrained and enriched with genuine insights and improved apprehensions as we follow out paths to aspects of the entities adumbrated in prehensions. Let us then say, on the foundation of the analogy between "perception" and "understanding" given above, that one may rightly assert the existence of a purported entity if one may direct one's thoughts to it, if one finds them thereby enriched with compelling insights into the entity, and if no hopeless imbroglio of confusion seems to stand in the way of an increasingly perfect and complete apprehension of the entity.

9. *Logical Investigations,* trans. J. N. Findlay (New York, 1970), vol. I, pp. 341–342.

This criterion—which, by the way, applies equally well to any category of objectivity (it is used in Chapter III to give a criterion for the justifiable assertibility of the existence of worlds)—gives the seeming objectivity or "reality" of abstract entities in our intellectual experience its due. If I read him correctly, it seems that Charles Peirce has proposed a similar criterion in his review of Berkeley's works.[10]

I have pointed out that the two main criteria deciding whether or not one is genuinely observing something objectual are (1) if one finds one's thoughts *constrained* when seeming to direct one's attention to the apparent object, and (2) if in so directing one's attention, one finds one's thoughts enriched, one finds oneself thinking things evidently, insightfully, clearly, compellingly true of the purported object. While it is true that there may be no sensory elements in nonvisual observation, this does not defeat our analogy between perceptual and nonperceptual observation. The reason becomes clear once one realizes that the sensory element in visual perception is one of the features of the sense-perceptual mode of observation which (1) has a constraining role and (2) has a fulfilling role, a role yielding enrichment of one's thoughts about the perceived object. One other function that the sensory element serves—at least according to some— is to make perceptual truth contingent upon physical truth. Of course, physical theory is not the last arbiter of perceptual truth, for physics is tied to, albeit underdetermined by, sense-perceptual observation. The point is that, although such a sensory element is lacking in, say, the observations of abstract objects, this does not entail that these are inadequate modes of observation; at worst it entails that physics has no analogous way of having anything to say about the truth of what is observed about abstract objects.

10. "Critical Review of Berkeley's Idealism," *Values in a Universe of Chance*, ed. P. P. Wiener (Garden City, N.Y., 1958), pp. 73–91.

In the observation of abstract objects such as proofs or mathematical entities, there are background theories which play the role of physics in the case of perceptual observations, viz., current logical theory in the first case and current mathematical theory in the second. Just as physical theory is parasitic on, in some measure dependent upon, sense-perceptual observation, so logic—at least in one view—is ultimately rooted in the study of arguments and their components, and mathematical theory is dependent upon particular mathematical studies. For example, a careful consideration of an argument may find it has a validity which current logical theory can't admit. A principal example is Hilbert's compelling use of classical reasoning to solve Gordan's Problem in the midst of prevailing constructivist logical "theory." Such an observation must, and did, disturb current logical practice, creating inevitable problems for logical theory.

What are the limitations of my concept of objective existence?

(1) It certainly seems to be the case that what is objectively existent is in some sense intersubjectively accessible—objectively existent entities somehow should not be accessible to one person only, they should not be in principle inaccessible to others. My concept of objective existence seems neutral toward the intersubjective existence of entities which are "objectively existent." My inclination is to trust an as yet not well-analyzed intuition I have that any experience rich and structured enough to justify asserting the "objective existence" of a purportedly experienced entity will have the compelling character of not being an experience strictly or essentially peculiar to me; thus the experience will have certain characteristics which I would be able to point to and convince myself that these are characteristics that experiences of other people could also have. These are the highly difficult issues Husserl begins to try to disentangle in the Fifth

Meditation of his *Cartesian Meditations*. There is a tantalizing mystery here; the problems are haunting. I do think, however, that, as soon as it is admitted that abstract entities have the kind of "objective existence" I claim for them, it will be difficult to dismiss them on the grounds that there is a great problem about their intersubjective character. I do not think that the extent and importance of the coincidence of the extensions of the concepts "existing independently of any particular person" and "in principle intersubjectively observable" are very well understood.

(2) There are important differences between our sensory perception of things and our "perception" of abstract objects. There is a certain truth to the claim that, when we first turn our attention to the problem of understanding the nature of objective existence, we take the perception of ordinary things as the paradigm in terms of which we try to understand forms of objective existence other than that of ordinary things. The greater the differences between sense-perceived objects and the objects presented in other modes of observation, the greater the tendency to feel uncomfortable with the latter and to slight the character of objective existence of the objects appearing in the latter modes. I have considerable trouble deciding what right we have finally to take visual perception as a paradigm. Consider some differences. In the case of visual perception there can be a failure of reference (hallucinations). There is a kind of "hallucination" in, say, mathematics—someone might give a false proof of the existence of a mathematical object which deceives everybody for years (this has happened, and is increasingly likely to happen for longer periods in this age of 200-page proofs). Physical or perceptual things are spatial, and we can relate to them as one physical object to another, while mathematical objects such as numbers or groups are not spatial, so there is literally no room to sustain the kind of reference that fails for percep-

tion in the case of hallucination. We are somehow made to feel uneasy about the mechanism of reference for abstract objects, and thus about the "objective existence" of abstract objects, seemingly because of the strong association we make between objectuality and physical concreteness. But does the absence of such concreteness in the case of abstract objects take away from the "objective existence" of abstract objects, or does this absence signify that we are considering another species of objectively existent entities? These are matters which require a great deal more thought (the reader is referred to Benacerraf's article "Mathematical Truth" for a discussion of some of the problems here in connection with the theory of reference). My conviction is that the criterion I have given for "objective existence" preserves what is essential for, say, scientific cognition, and maybe for truth. Its power is "to preserve the appearance," categorizing objectuality, rather than reducing it to, say, physical reality. Some might also think this its weakness. If the unparsimonious, antireductive character is somehow found offensive on such grounds, at least this much can still be said on its behalf: by taking seriously the "objective existence" of entities affirmed by the criterion given above, one achieves an understanding of the fullest range of apparent "objective domains," "worlds," which must be eliminated reductively if one is, e.g., a physicalist.

I.2. Frege and Ego-Independent Truth-Bearers

I will now present the essentials of Frege's reflections on the objectuality of intensional entities in his article "The Thought." [11] The point of this section is to learn from Frege that from the lowest cognitive levels of sense-perception

11. Bracketed numbers in this section refer to pages of the article.

to the highest cognitive levels of the justification of theories, ego-independent intensional entities or, at least, ego-independent truth-bearers of some kind, are required if we are to have access to an ego-independent, perfectly external world.

A *thought* is something for which the question of truth arises; for Frege it is the *Sinn* of a sentence, and such sentences are said to express thoughts. I will use the term 'truth-bearer' instead of 'thought' when I wish to be neutral on the matter of what truth-bearers might be, whether they be, e.g., propositions, *Sinne,* beliefs, eternal sentences, judgments. 'Thinking' refers to the apprehension of a thought, and 'judgment' refers to the recognition of the truth of a thought; 'assertions' refer to public manifestations of judgments [22].

Frege argues that thoughts are objective or objectual. The argument rests on two grounds: a circumscription of the subjective and the intentionality of consciousness.

Totally subjective, ego-dependent entities are called 'ideas'; ideas are sense-impressions, sensations, feelings, moods, inclinations, wishes, and the like [26]. Frege argues that thoughts are not ideas and that they are not things. Thoughts are like things in that they are independent of ideas and unlike things in that they are not sense-perceivable [28–29]. Therefore, thoughts must form a third world or realm [29].

Here is his argument for the difference between things and ideas [26–28]. Ideas can not be sense-perceived; things can. Ideas are "had" or, perhaps one can say, suffered; otherwise they don't exist (they are ego-dependent). A thing exists whether or not I am perceiving it; a perception of a tree exists only if it is suffered or had. Ideas need a bearer—there is a unique conscious being who has an idea. Things are independent of consciousness and do not need a bearer. Ideas can refer to things outside of ideas, viz., to physical things, to that lime tree there. Two persons can have (necessarily distinct) ideas referring to the same thing.

It is worth remarking that a person's ideas may readily be interpreted as the content of what Husserl calls "the sphere of the actuality and potentialities of the stream of subjective processes" which comes into view under phenomenological reflection, under the shift from the natural focus (on a or "the" world) to the transcendental focus (on the stream of experience, of consciousness).

So, on first analysis, things are not ideas. Are thoughts ideas? Frege considers the Pythagorean theorem. It would be wrong to speak of *my* Pythagorean theorem [28]. Well, at least it seems wrong. One must look closely to see why what at first seems wrong *is* wrong. Earlier in the article Frege argues that thoughts are truth-bearers. He now points out that if, say, 'red' characterized *only* something internal, something totally ego-dependent, then it would be applicable only to my ideas; then, by analogy, if 'true' characterized only something internal, then truth would be restricted to my ideas [29]. But if my ideas were true—remember that my ideas can never be anyone else's ideas—then there could be no science common to many, for science demands shared truths. "No contradiction between any sciences of different persons would then be possible and it would really be idle to dispute about truth [29]."

Suppose that all references beyond ideas were illusory, that "all things" are truly only ideas.

Does a shell weighing a hundred kilogrammes exist, according to this view? Perhaps, but I could know nothing of it. If a shell is not my idea then, according to our thesis, it cannot be an object of awareness, of my thinking. But if a shell were my idea, it would have no weight. I can have an idea of a heavy shell. This then contains the idea of weight as a part-idea. But this part-idea is not a property of the whole any more than Germany is a property of Europe. So it follows:

Either the thesis that only what is my idea can be the object of my awareness is false, or all my knowledge and perception is limited to the range of my ideas, to the stage of my consciousness. In this case I should have only an inner world and I should know nothing of other people. [30–31]

These arguments are now repeated with a twist and on a grander scale. The insight described by the title of this section, which has already been intimated above, now emerges with force. Frege may be construed as giving a phenomenological/intentional analysis of the natural attitude, of the nature of the ascriptions in our ordinary and special prehensions of the natural world and other external worlds.

Consider a physiologist of the senses. What follows now parallels [31–32]. Far from supposing that the things he touches and sees are ideas, he believes that his sense-impressions give him the surest proof that there are things wholly independent of his ideas, things which have no need of consciousness. Suppose that he traces the physical chain beginning with light rays, through nervous tissues, ending with ideas. Similar ideas may have quite different physical beginnings. My having an idea of a tree does not require a tree to be before me. Thus the content of ideas seems to be independent of the physical origins of the ideas. Furthermore, the stimulation behind an idea is not actually itself immediately given, but is only a hypothesis. "If we call what happens in our consciousness idea, then we really only experience ideas, but not their causes. . . . If a scientist wants to avoid all mere hypothesis, then only ideas are left for him." The light rays, the nerve fibers, etc., resolve into ideas. So he finally undermines his own science. Is indeed everything idea? That is, does everything need "a bearer" for stability? Is everything ego-dependent? But "is it not strange how the opposites [now] collapse into one another?"—for just as the reduction of things to ideas leads to the collapse of the physiologist's science, it also leads to the explosion of the notion of ideas. Ideas need a bearer, but if everything is an idea, the bearer must be an idea. But then why not choose, say, this idea which is a chair rather than that idea which is a human being, as a bearer? "Why, after all, have a bearer for ideas at all?"

But in fact the physiologist does not confuse the nerve cell with the sensations, the doctor does not confuse the patient's pain with his own. "So, it seems to me, the matter becomes intelligible. If man could not think and could not take something to be the bearer of his thought he would have an inner world but no outer world. . . . Not everything that can be the object of my understanding is an idea. . . . [Otherwise] the natural sciences too could only be assessed as fables" [34].

In a certain respect, Frege seems to assume what he wants to demonstrate. The point about his arguments, however, is that he is trying not to prove something to us, but to reveal something. The force of Frege's arguments clearly depends on respecting the integrity of what Husserl would call 'systems of intentionality', which we may roughly construe as conceptual systems having the character of referring to objects of an external domain, or, better, as *all of the ascriptions of an object to be found in one's prehensions, one's apprehension, of the object.* In each case Frege shows that the reduction or proposed reduction of "external objects" to ideas explodes such systems of intentionalities, or goes against what is ascribed to the purported objects in even the most fundamental elements of one's prehensions, creating massive inconsistencies and absurdities.

Of course, these observations do not *prove* that the objects referred to by systems of intentionalities in prehensions exist. Frege's point is, I think, rather different and in the main

Husserlian. Respecting the integrity of the elements of such systems (insofar as they manifest such integrity) is a necessary condition for having an external world and a self. Of course, mistakes do happen—

By the step with which I secure an environment for myself [viz., by respecting the integrity of systems of intentionality, of the ascriptions made in my prehensions of objects] I expose myself to the risk of error. . . . Doubt never altogether leaves us in our excursions into the outer world. [But] it is difficult to distinguish probability from certainty here, so we can presume to judge about things in the outer world. And we must presume this even at the risk of error if we do not want to succumb to far greater dangers. [34]

Let us try to clarify the relation between external objects, ideas, and thoughts (truth-bearers). If things are not to be ideas, there must be something in or along side of our ideas which refers beyond ideas.

We have visual impressions, not only not the same, but markedly different from each other. And yet we move about in the same outer world. Having visual impressions is certainly necessary for seeing things but not sufficient. What must be added is non-sensible. *And yet* this is just what opens up the outer world for us; for without this nonsensible something everyone would remain shut up in his inner world. [36]

This element, the nonsensible something, a thought, a truth-bearer, must be independent of any particular idea if it is to be capable of being used to frame an external world. Frege has shown that things cannot be ideas *if* certain systems of intentionalities are to make sense, for those systems of intentionalities "speak" of external, ego-independent entities (e.g., physical things in the external world). Frege also argued that thoughts, the components of what I have referred to as 'systems of intentionalities', truth-bearers, must also be ego-independent, independent of my ideas, of the immanent formations of *my* stream of consciousness. If 'true', he says, characterized only ideas, then truth would be restricted to ideas. But this, too, conflicts with the systems of intentionalities framing, e.g., the external physical world, the domain of Euclidean geometry, or the world of prices. The framing ascriptions in the relevant prehensions, the framing systems of intentionalities, "speak" on behalf of the worlds they frame being there for anyone, being there determinately whether or not anyone wishes or wills them to be there, whether or not anyone is having ideas or experiences, and they "speak" against what is true of them being true only here and now, for this idea, this ego, this frame of mind or feeling or sensation. To the extent that a thought is dependent for its truth upon the immanent contents of an ego's stream of experience, to that extent is the world it frames clearly dependent upon that ego, and to the same extent the framed, prehended, world does not endure beyond those phases of the ego's experiences and so is not a truly external, truly ego-independent world.

These considerations may be summed up in two observations:

Observation 1. Our prehensions (prehensive apprehensions) of "the external world" contain ascriptions construing the world as independent of any particular ego's ideas, of any particular ego's stream of experience. (This is the result of so-to-speak *phenomenological* reflection, reflection on consciousness, on the relevant prehensions and the so-called "systems of intentionalities," complexes of ascriptions, in them.)

Observation 2. To the extent that truth-bearers are independent as far as their truth is concerned of any ego's ideas or experience, to that extent they may frame an ego-independent, external world. Independent truth-bearers are required in order rightly or soundly to frame an ego-independent, truly external, objective domain or world.

By way of clarifying the second observation, let us explore some ways in which truth-bearers might be ego-dependent. While Frege argued in effect that there must be independent truth-bearers if we are to have access to an external, ego-independent world, he of course has not proved that such things exist. In a certain respect, deciding this issue is one of the great problems of modern philosophy and logic. What Frege and Husserl saw is how this problem is important even at the level of understanding the simplest orders of sense-perception.

I will now briefly examine some of the more familiar ways in which truth-bearers might be ego-dependent.

1. My assertion "this is a madman," if a truth-bearer at all, is an ego-dependent truth-bearer; it must be supplemented by an act pointing to or otherwise indicating which person I have in mind. Worlds that can be referred to or framed only by the use of 'this' (as in "this world"), because they thus depend on an ego-dependent truth-bearer, are ego-dependent.

2. Consider the theorem that there is at least one prime number, and for every prime number there is a greater prime number. A nonconstructive mathematician would regard this theorem as highly ego-independent. It says what is either true or false independently of whether anyone has decided it. A constructivist, or, better, an intuitionist, would regard the theorem as incomplete, as an ego-dependent truth-bearer not unlike the assertion "this is a madman." It becomes complete, or completely intelligible, only when proof or disproof is given. Thus, the world of intuitionistic mathematics is ego-dependent, but it is not entirely so, for it is limited by the field of possible or potential truth-bearers, possible or poten-

tial undecided theorems. Furthermore, if Husserl is right about the nature of abstraction (see his *Logical Investigations,* Investigations II, III), then, indeed, even a Brouwerian intuitionist [12] must grant that there are ego-independent abstract entities, e.g., Brouwer's abstract "two-ity," or the laws of construction. Indeed, it is surely an "intuitive" certainty that not everything goes in the intuitionist universe; there is some ego-independent, abstract and intelligible, intuitable "order" conditioning what is constructible; otherwise, for instance, Brouwer could never have begun.

3. Quine has argued that there are no Fregean truth-bearers,[13] or that the best we can do by way of having independent truth-bearers are eternal sentences. But the usual reflections on how genuinely "eternal" an eternal sentence is will reveal to us something of the nature of their dependence. Quine's holistic view of language, his view of the way that "dictionary" merges with "encyclopedia," predestines a strong element of noneternality in eternal sentences. Clearly, the Pythagorean theorem has changed in "meaning" from the time of the Pythagoreans. One suspects they thought they were proving something about space. Today, the "theorem" is used as a postulate to distinguish Euclidean manifolds from manifolds having other metrics (e.g., the surface of a torus). That is, we now realize that its truth is dependent on the kind of manifold being considered. So the seemingly eternal sentence(s) the Greeks used to state the theorem must be extended to include reference to the manifold at issue, something they could not have conceived of as necessary. On a different tack, James Thomson has argued [14] that one can

12. See, e.g., L. E. J. Brouwer, "Historical Background, Principles and Methods of Intuitionism," *South African Journal of Science,* 49 (1952), 139–146.

13. *Philosophy of Logic* (Englewood Cliffs, N.J., 1970), chap. 1.

14. "Truth-Bearers and the Trouble about Propositions," *Journal of Philosophy.* 66 (1969), 737–747.

never be certain that all ambiguities are completely elemi-
nated from an eternal sentence, no matter how carefully it
has been expanded. Consider—

If one does *explain* truth in terms of our talk of a world [15]
(e.g., "Snow is white" is true if and only if snow is white),
then the uncontainable threat of ambiguity, shift of "meaning," or vagueness makes of truth a shaky affair (because
truth was explained in terms of essentially shaky language;
truth, and therefore its objective correlate, the world, become
shaky). That is, the ambiguity, vagueness, or changeableness
of "meaning" are transmitted through the truth predicate
and infect the world (otherwise truth comes apart from being,
but then the purpose of "truth," to say how the world is, is
lost).

I.3. The Observability of Abstract Entities and the Problem of Analytic Truth

I wish to discuss these matters in order to make contact
with some issues arising here, but without going into detail
on this occasion. I will consider a few ways in which the problem of linguistic meaning and the possibility of the observation of, and therefore the existence of, abstract entities fail
to have, at least a priori, much to do with one another.

Some would claim that any adequate theory of meaning
should carry with it an adequate, effective theory of translation. The observability of intensional entities—if such there
be—does not, however, carry with it any special assurance
that effective criteria for the existence and identity of intensional entities are or need be forthcoming, as we know from

15. Alfred Tarski, "The Concept of Truth in Formalized Languages,"
in *Logic, Semantics, Metamathematics*, trans. J. H. Woodger (Oxford,
1956), pp. 152–279.

the history of the observability of other sorts of abstract entities, viz., magnitudes, as discussed at the beginning of this chapter. We have to be sure, given a criterion for their existence, but it does not a priori seem a criterion helpful in matters of an effective theory of translation when applied to expressions for intensional entities.

In "On What There Is" in *From a Logical Point of View,* Quine introduces personae who introduce abstract entities or intensional entities to explain, or to justify interpretations of, certain affairs of assertion. He finds ways of treating the affairs obviating the need for such entities. If McX argues from the fact that there are red houses, red roses, red sunsets, to the claim that there is an attribute denoted by 'red', Quine counters by arguing that we can just say that the predicate 'red' is *true of* such red things; nothing is gained by making red an attribute. Or McX argues that, even if 'red' does not denote an attribute, it is surely meaningful. Thus it has associated with it a meaning. Quine counters by pointing out that we can make sense of meaningfulness without recourse to meanings, viz., we can analyze significance in terms of behavior (a project fully begun in Quine's *Word and Object*).

I do not think that Quine really argues point blank that there aren't meanings, but only that whatever needs they fill or seem to satisfy can usually be satisfied better by talk of something nonintensional. In both cases just considered I certainly follow Quine. I wouldn't think of introducing abstract entities on such grounds, or for such purposes. It is doubtful that McX had a sufficient grasp on the entities he tried to introduce to satisfy my criterion for asserting their existence. It is not inconceivable, provided our purposes are not corrupt (like McX's), that we could find that there are genuinely intensional entities, that we could think about them, and that our thought could move toward an increasingly rich and compelling understanding of them. The examples of "observed" abstract entities (from Weyl and Gödel) show this could be so. These examples were not inspired by McXian considerations. One can have abstract and even intensional entities while heeding the caveat issuing from Quine's writings about the impotency of assuming such things for the sake of an effective theory of meaningfulness. Even if one finds, on the foundation of our phenomenological criterion for their existence, that intensional entities exist, it may be that there are better paths toward a theory of translation. But this does not free us to assert their nonexistence; at best it frees us to ignore intensional entities insofar as translation is important to us.

Let us assume that intensional entities are observable and so exist. I wish to consider briefly the attitude toward "analytic truth" shaped by this assumption. I want to say that nothing is true by meaning alone. I will later argue that even so-called "logical laws" are not "true by meaning." These are positions for which Quine has argued vigorously. The main point is that I may observe that something is the case but be required neither to explain why it is the case nor to suppose that there is a why-explanation. Consider: Suppose that by looking behind him I observe that there isn't a lobster following Sartre. My observation is sufficient grounds for asserting what I observe. It is very difficult to imagine what a good why-explanation would be like in this case.

Husserl, in his extended phenomenological analyses of acts directed toward, say, colors considered *"in specie,"* makes it clear that even a purported entity like "redness," which is so bare of significant determinations and so close to material intuition (in contrast, say, to the example from Weyl, viz., "symmetry"), has enough "content" or aspects to sustain compelling thoughts, e.g., that red is extended (cf., for example, his *Logical Investigations,* Investigations I and II). I find, by

the kinds of observations produced by the kinds of intellectual exercises described by Husserl, that I am compelled to
agree that colors are extended. I do not claim that this is an
immutable truth any more than I would claim that there
wasn't a lobster following Sartre was an immutable truth.
Further observation and insight may prove me wrong, as
people were wrong about, say, the nature of dimension until
Poincaré and Brouwer gave their analyses.[16] In the last case
it was clearly "observed" that the analysis of dimension is
correct, e.g., by proving that the dimension of Euclidean
n-space is n.

Just as it would be difficult to say why it is true that there
was no lobster following Sartre, so it would be difficult to
say why it is true that red is extended. I clearly would not
want to say that 'color is extended' is "true by meaning."
I *insightfully* grasp its truth by an extended exercise of intellective and sensory imagination. The integrity of such an
observation is just as strong as the integrity of my observation
that there was no lobster following Sartre (going back to the
original analogy between perception and the observation of
abstract entities in I.1 for the sense of 'as strong as' here).
An observation to the effect that all bachelors are unmarried
men, or to the effect that red is extended, in contrast to
Weyl's extended analysis of, observation of, the nature of
symmetry, is not a good paradigm, for it is too shallow to
admit instructive appreciation. Talk of observation becomes
compelling in the case of the analysis of symmetry, and so
becomes compelling derivatively in the former case. One
must remember that even in the case of visual perception it
is sometimes hard to tell whether one has genuinely observed
something or whether one is simply giving voice to habits of
mind.

16. See, e.g., the Introduction of W. Hurewicz and H. Wallman,
Dimension Theory (Princeton, N.J., 1948).

II | Phenomena

A *concept,* if such a thing exists, is an intensional entity referring to an entity or to a class of entities. A person's *conception* of an entity is quite another matter. From my point of view, a person's conception of an entity, viz., *my* conception, is the principal goal of ("naive") phenomenological analysis. My conception is a phenomenon; it determines how the entity "appears" to me. A *concept* is the intensional correlate of an *essence.* It is a remarkable phenomenological fact of our intellectual and perceptual experience that conceptions often do the work of concepts, viz., they sometimes frame or fix the entity, making of it a stable goal of cognitive pursuit. This chapter, the next, and the Appendix, examine this remarkable fact. In this chapter I say what a conception is and show how it forms the foundation for the construction of increasingly sound theories of the object. The next chapter digs somewhat more deeply into this last matter, yielding a kind of phenomenological ontology.

I will not be able to give a precise explanation of "*p*'s conception of such and such." But I believe that I will be able to say enough to fix *conceptions* as genuine objects of philosophical/phenomenological research. The novelty of phenomenology—or phenomenology under my conception as the study of conceptions, of "phenomena" understood as conceptions—is that of making such things objects of philosophic study and especially of studying them in the respects discussed in this chapter and the next. The Appendix relates phenomenology so construed to Husserl's phenomenology. I will now give an increasingly precise explanation of what I count as a conception of something.

I find my attention fixed on some prehended object. Keeping the object fixed, I can, by reflection, discern and gather together all of my thoughts, doubts, beliefs, perceptions, theories, etc., that in any way concern or seem to concern the object. These are parts of my *conception* of the fixed object; alternatively speaking, they together constitute a *phenomenon* determining how the object "appears" to me. (I prefer the idiom of "conception," but use the idiom of "appear" and "phenomenon" for the sake of historical associations.)

What is immediately noticeable about a conception of something is how disparate its elements may be. E.g., I can, without realizing it, believe contradictory things about the same object, or I can have perceptions of the object whose relations to one another as perceptions of the same thing are not at all clear. A fully justified theory of an object represents a very special and unusual element in a conception—when it exists at all. The best of such theories are set forth on the foundation of one's having gone through all of the elements of his conception and having decided how they should contribute to the theory, what their cognitive worth is. Only on the foundation of such a theory does one's conception acquire an explicit logical unity and only on such a foundation is it clear what all the elements have to do with one another.

I will now give an example of a conception, on the basis of which I will be able to offer a more precise explanation of "*p*'s conception of such and such." I fix my attention on the horsetail tree standing in front of the Philosophy Corner at

Stanford. Here are some of the elements of my conception that I reflectively notice.

I see that it is a tree.

I know on good authority that it is an Australian horsetail tree.

I see that it is solid, tall.

I see that it has another side.

I suspect that the other side is much like the one facing me.

I notice that the bark is grey.

I notice that many of the branches hang down in a way suggestive of a horse's tail.

I see that it has long needles instead of leaves.

What I can see of the needles suggests that they are like pine needles.

I see that the branches are tightly clustered with small black objects.

I conjecture that the small black objects are like pine cones.

I now walk closer to the tree and around it.

I see that I am closer to the same tree and that I am looking at it more closely, seeing it more closely.

I now see that the needles are rather different from pine needles.

I see that the needles are segmented and find that they are brittle.

I observe that the needles are formed somewhat like reeds; they seem as primitive.

I see that the black objects are more like nuts than pine cones, although they are woody like pine cones and seem to be open.

This list barely scratches the surface of my conception of the horsetail tree. None of my aesthetic perceptions and emotional, even sentimental, associations are mentioned. Furthermore, the descriptions are quite crude. There are many delicate differences among the mental acts hidden beneath the boringly repeated term 'see that'.

Notice that the conception grew and changed in time, later judgments "correcting" earlier judgments. One must add as elements of my conception second and higher order judgments (judgments about judgments) such as

I see that I was wrong when I conjectured that it was like a pine tree, although there is a striking resemblance.

I see that I was right in saying that (believing that) I saw a tree.

At its simplest level, "phenomenological analysis" consists of no more than gathering together and adequately expressing the elements of a conception.

With this example of a conception as background, let us see if we can specify *conceptions* more closely than we have. A conception is always associated with some one conscious, thinking, and experiencing self p. A conception is determined by p's fixing (by a prehension) on some object or seeming-object o, and, on the foundation of his fix on the object, his gathering together such acts of consciousness, of experience and thought, as have been illustrated above. We may reasonably take a prehension of o as the element in p's experience that fixes on o. Call the selected prehension 'i' and the object or seeming-object fixed upon 'o_i' or simply 'o'. Let $s(i)$ be any sentence that directly or indirectly concerns, e.g., mentions, o_i. We should fix a period of time t in order to have control over what otherwise would be an extremely unwieldy entity.

The taking of i to be a prehension of o_i is motivated by an important property of prehensions that emerged in our previous studies, viz., in adumbrating further aspects of o_i, they provide the means to identify further prehensions, apprehensions, of o_i as "further apprehensions of the same thing." A conception as determined by p, t, and i does not then contain everything in p's experience relating to o_i, for p may *in fact* be in some instance perceiving o_i but not be able to see that he is doing so on the basis of i.

A conception (p,t,i) is fully determined by the collection of all true statements of the following form which could be ideally recognized by p (not necessarily during t) as being true (during t) of p. Note that different occurrences of $s(i)$ below may represent different sentences, although it is assumed that i is fixed and that the sentences are recognizable, by some chain of considerations, as being in some sense about i, and so recognized ultimately on the foundation of i. (Recall the previous examples of the observation of a tree and the observation of an argument and how, on the foundation of an initial prehension i or o_i, further observations were recognized as being observations of o_i—this is a theme that will be developed more fully, especially in the next chapter.)

p sees that $s(i)$.

p believes that $s(i)$.

p doubts that $s(i)$.

p sees that $s(i)$ can be proved.

p sees that $s(i)$ can be proved by such and such a means.

p hypothesizes that $s(i)$ upon such and such grounds.

p sees o_i and, on the grounds of that seeing, perceives that $s(i)$.

p remembers that $s(i)$.

p has verified that $s(i)$ in such and such a way.

p desires that $s(i)$.

p sees that $s(i)$ is probably true.

p sees that such and such an observation can verify that $s(i)$.

p has an insight into o_i to the effect that $s(i)$.

And so on. It must be kept in mind that some statements can be much more complex than those just illustrated—perhaps of the complexity required in order to express one's grounds for accepting a full scientific theory of o_i, $s(i)$ expressing such a theory. Also, some of the statements may be of second order or higher, e.g., judgments about judgments. Some statements may contain an extremely refined, elaborate, and highly nuanced description of the mental acts involved.

Let us symbolize the expressions of the sort listed or indicated by the list above. Expressions of the form '$\Delta(p,s(i),b)$' will be used, where '$\Delta(\ldots,\ldots,\ldots)$' in each case expresses, e.g., ' . . . sees that . . . ', ' . . . has verified that . . . ', ' . . . has the insight to the effect that . . . ', ' . . . sees that is probably true . . . '. The 'b' carries the weight of what is left in the expressions besides the 'p' and the '$s(i)$', e.g., the 'can be proved' or the 'upon such and such grounds'. Exactly how a sentence expressing the elements of a conception should be parsed in order to bring it into the form '$\Delta(p,s(i),b)$' is equivocal; but this will do us no harm, for it is not intended that the Δ-expressions should represent a logical analysis of the considered statements, but only that they should remind us of the typical vital parts of such statements. (The expressions of the form '$\Delta(p,s(i),b)$' are called "delta-sentences.") I have already given an example of a partial analysis of the conception (myself; the afternoon of July 9, 1975, at about 2 P.M.; my perceptual prehension of the horsetail tree).

If the reader now returns to the example from Gödel given in the Introduction, I think he will be able to see more precisely why I called it 'phenomenological analysis', for Gödel was there unraveling a *conception* of the universe of set theory.

I will now consider some of the most obvious roles that the analysis of phenomena plays in finding the solution of intellectual problems and the construction of scientific theories.

(a) It is obvious that conceptions receive much attention in our intellectual and scientific work. The current conception determined by i contains p's current theories about o_i, as well as his relevant observations, insights, intuitions, etc., about o_i, improving his current best theory.

(b) A primary intellectual task is that of gathering together the elements of a conception and of discovering "rational order" in those contents, for when p seeks to solve problems about o_i or to improve his understanding of o_i, p *must* begin with analyses of his thoughts about, insights into, intuitions concerning, perceptions of, theories about, . . . , o_i. Gathering together the elements of his conception in an effort to perfect his conception logically is indeed the second step in solving any scientific problem (the first is to understand the problem).[1]

(c) Conceptions are the principal focus of a familiar and painful kind of intellectual labor—that of transforming a private, unarticulated insight or intuition into a public, reasoned theory.

I will give two simple examples, to illustrate the observation that, typically, when one goes through the elements of a sufficiently rich, but not as yet explicitly, logically unified conception of some object or world, it will typically happen that an intuitive logical unity among those elements, and thus a scientific theory, will begin to emerge. The second example is slightly more detailed.

Example 1. The following is an imaginary, highly fragmentary analysis of a phenomenon (p,t,i), $p = $ a biologist, $t = $ some period of time in, say, the sixteenth century, $o_i = $ the natural world and the life within it. (Perhaps i is some perception of living things together with certain vague recollections of past experiences of such things.)[2] The following is

1. G. Polya, *How to Solve It* (Princeton, 1945), chap. 1.

2. This example is crudely drawn from François Jacob, *The Logic of Life* (New York, 1973). This history of genetics is phenomenological in tone.

a principal element in (p,t,i) having the complexity of a theory (I have allowed for such elements in the explanation of (p,t,i)). I will present it informally; my point is not so subtle that I need to use explicit Δ-sentences.

"Surely, considerations of any particular thing must reveal an entity composed of matter and form. Don't we have the testimony of the ancients on this matter? Any man of faith must agree that it is ultimately through God's guidance that Nature confers form on matter. One must infer from this that the powerful and suggestive system of resemblances among things is there by God's will and for the sake of his divine purposes. Thus the visible networks of analogues and similitudes provide access to Nature's, and therefore God's, secrets. Thanks to these similitudes and signatures, the invisible becomes visible. For example, as any man can see, all parts of plants correspond to parts of animals; roots are similar to mouths, leaves to hair, wood to bone, veins to veins, and so on. What better ground than this strong resemblance could we have for locating the vital principle of the plant where stem joints root, for the heart occurs in the corresponding place in man. Or, also—are not all living animals possessed of heat? Is not heat necessary for the generation of life? (Just look around you to see how the heat belongs to the living but not the dead.) Heat is thus a vital part of all living beings. And—the resemblance between fathers and sons is surely no accident. It must indeed be that the drop of seed from which we are produced bears in itself the impression of the bodily shapes, and of the thoughts and inclinations, of our fathers."

One can readily see that in p's case there was a time s before t such that (p,s,i) was full of scattered and unorganized, but deeply impressive and disturbing, observations of similarities among a wide spectrum of beings and processes, as well as not infrequent legends and observations of sympathies among such similar entities. By brooding over such things through the lens of his faith, p discerned the "logical" order noted above in those scattered observations among the elements of (p,s,i), and the little theory or theories given above emerged.

Example 2. Let us now consider (p,t,i) where $p =$ myself, $t =$ the present, $o_i =$ where I am now, and $i =$ my current perception of myself in the world about me.

I ask myself the question: Where am I now? i is a prehension of my position. But in trying to give a definite answer to the question, I find that my mind is crowded with a confusion of certainties—I am in the university library, I am twenty feet from where I was twenty minutes ago, I am two miles southeast of my apartment, and so on. I am also aware that my position is changing in relation to the sun and in relation to that person walking toward the stacks. Instead of having one answer to my question, I find that I have many answers. None of them fully satisfies me, although each seems in some way correct. All these answers contribute to my current conception of my position; but there is a clear need to evaluate each as a statement of my position, to discover the inner logical unity, if there is one, which gives them all the character of stating my position. The hope is that going with care through the elements of (p,t,i) will result in a better apprehension of o_i and perhaps an understanding of the nature of position in abstraction from this particular position.

The reader may imagine my going through the elements of (p,t,i), trying to find some unity among them. At last I notice that in each case I have fixed upon an object which I use to generate "a frame of reference," determining in relation to that object where I am now by locating myself in terms of a directed distance from that object; o_i and, indeed, the nature of position, are thus better apprehended. I can now begin to develop a theory of position, of "frames of reference."

If I am bold and imaginative, I may be led to raise deep questions such as "Is there an absolute frame of reference?" or, "Do physical laws vary as one varies frames of reference?"

The emerging understanding of a frame of reference, determined throughout by the contents or elements of my conception (p,t,i) of my position, helped to yield an understanding of the underlying unity of those contents, a unity not apprehended until I had undertaken a phenomenological analysis and brooded over the result. Such brooding led by harmonious phases of understanding to the conception of frames of reference. To have arbitrarily imposed a structure on the elements of the phenomenon, the conception, would not have been rational; it would have been madness. The choice of structure had to be motivated and regulated throughout by the elements of the conception. To the extent that important "principles" become apprehensible on the foundation of closer analysis of the elements of phenomena, thus yielding a logical unity in them and so a better apprehension of o_i, to that extent are elements of arbitrariness and conventionality eliminated from our emergent theory of o_i. In this way at least, phenomena or conceptions regulate our understanding of o_i and form the grounds on which our understanding must be established. Thus, in a sense, phenomenological analysis is the beginning of thought.

Speaking generally, phenomena or conceptions are important to us because they are the foundation on which we base knowledge and understanding, deeper cognitive apprehension, of the apparent entity o. Since the phenomenon or conception contains all in one's experience that has to do with o, the phenomenon must be regulative of what counts as knowledge and understanding of o. Unless we fully understand the phenomenon associated with o_i, unless we fully understand all in our experience and thought that determines what counts as knowledge and understanding of o, we are likely, in our cognitive pursuit, to lose the intended, orginally prehended entity and so have a false theory or understanding of it. In our study of prehension we have already seen how, on the foundation of adumbrations in the prehension, the prehension is regulative of further cognitive apprehension of *o*. We have seen a variation of this theme emerge in the above examples, as logical unities among the elements of a conception are adumbrated in the phenomenological analysis of the conception. This element of adumbration is the foundation of our further apprehension of *o* and so must be considered. The next chapter examines this, and especially its philosophic consequences, in more detail.

III | A Fundamental Fact of Intellectual Experience

It would seem that a conception (p,t,i) is an entirely subjective affair, like a Fregean idea. This is rather paradoxical in view of the fact that, because of the very comprehensiveness of a conception (p,t,i), some conception must form the foundation from which we have access to an objective world. A metaphysics that strains to consider objects on the one hand and conceptions on the other and seeks to justify claims to cognition on the basis of "real" connections between conceptions and objects misses a serious point (mainly a Husserlian point), viz., that at some time one must assume the validity of some core of *some* conception and on this foundation one must establish "real" relations between conceptions and objects. One must begin with some conception. Descartes, for example, may be viewed as having attempted to seek out such a founding conception. Husserl sought to make the products of "transcendental reflection" on "transcendental subjectivity" such a founding conception.

To seek out and clearly define such fundamental conceptions is a difficult but not altogether unrewarding task. Quite independently of such foundational or radical research, however, it would be extremely useful to learn how or in what ways *any* conception (p,t,i) can serve as a foundation for cognition of its object o_i. The fundamental thesis I propose, a thesis already presented in the Introduction and enriched somewhat in Chapter II is this—insofar as a conception (p,t,i) genuinely or validly posits an object o_i, it must yield an understanding of what further experiences and observations can, if achieved, enrich p's cognitive apprehension of o_i. This understanding must be yielded on the foundation of adumbrations in i or succeeding apprehensions referring back to i. In this chapter I will explain further how and in what sense conceptions sustain such apprehensions. When they fail to do so it must be said that the conceptions are inadequate, that they fail to rightly or validly posit their purported object o_i.

What will emerge is that, in spite of a conception being in each case "my conception," conceptions sometimes contain or sustain a core of understanding (to be called '$Val(p,t,i)$') strongly independent of p's will and desire, establishing the "objectivity" or "reality" of the purported object o_i.

III.1. On $Val(p,t,i)$: A Source of Authority in our Thought

The chapter title refers to this fundamental "phenomenological" fact of intellectual experience: When we think about an object o_i, an understanding invariably develops not only of the object, but also of what considerations and observations (what mental states, what acts of consciousness) will decide questions about the object. More precisely, when we go through the elements of a conception (p,t,i) with a view to accrediting and improving them, an understanding that I will henceforth call '$Val(p,t,i)$' emerges; this is an understanding of what mental events, if actualized, would yield better apprehensions of o_i, e.g., justifiable assertions about o_i.

$Val(p,t,i)$ may be thought of as analyzable in terms of

second order Δ-sentences, Δ-sentences wherein $s(i)$ is a Δ-sentence, of the form

p sees that (sees with insight that) if $\Delta(p,s(i),b)$ is true, then
p may justifiably assert that $s(i)$.

Recall that the truth of a Δ-sentence entails or requires the existence of a certain mental event, e.g., p sees that . . . , p has perceived that . . . , p has proved that . . . , p remembers that . . . .

I will now present some examples that are continuations of previous examples. These purport to analyze conceptions, to be phenomenological analyses. It seems unnecessary to put them into the form of Δ-sentences.

Example 1. Let $p =$ myself, $t =$ the present, and $i =$ my current perception of a jar full of stones standing before me. Suppose I set myself the task of further apprehending the jar of stones; to be specific, suppose I set myself the task of determining how many stones are in the jar.

I see before me a jar filled with small stones. The jar looks completely full. I set myself the task of counting the stones in the jar. I realize that in order to count them with complete accuracy I must remove them from the jar one by one, assigning the number '1' to the first stone I take out and the respective successive cardinal number to each successive stone. I see that I can get closer to the jar and that the closer I get the more clearly will I be able to see the jar and the stones inside. I see that I will then be able to reach inside the jar and remove the stones one by one.

Notice that, by examining the contents of my perceptual field containing the jar and by considering what it means to count something, I can see how to trace a course of physical acts that will lead to a course of mental acts successfully presenting me with a more determinate view of the jar and its contents, allowing me in the end to say with justification how many stones are in the jar. The content and nature of the field of perception, which includes a perception of myself as a thinking, wandering psycho-physical being who can move closer to things as well as my understanding that my perception of a thing can be improved by moving nearer to it, sustains the insight that I could by such and such means produce further perceptions of the jar and its contents. These perceptions would indeed be better, more complete, and more determinate presentations of "the same thing." By in this way brooding over the elements of the conceptions, the phenomenon, (p,t,i), those elements so contemplated thus inspire and sustain or fulfill certain accrued insights into how to cognitively apprehend the jar better and more completely.

Clearly and simply in the manner just indicated, gathering together and brooding over the elements of (p,t,i) on the foundation of the initial prehension i (elements that included the relevant "perceptions" of the jar, myself, etc.) produced an increasingly sharp and complete understanding $Val\ (p,t,i)$ of how to cognitively apprehend the jar more completely. Notice how these element of conceptions converged and overlapped harmoniously to produce these understandings: my understanding of myself, of my possibilities for movement, of how movement alters my perception, of what it is for something to be a jar full of stones, of what it is to count, of what it is to move about in order to perceive something more completely and more closely, of how moving closer to the jar alters my perceptions of the jar but does not alter the jar, of how the continuous phases of my perception of the jar as I move about it are continuously altered and in certain ways become improved perceptions of "the same thing," of the fact that the spatial closeness to our eyes of an object does indeed produce a better and more determinate perception of detailed features of the object. The way these understandings harmonize with one another, flow into one another, and reinforce one another, yields, on the foundation of (p,t,i), a fully compelling and insightful understanding $Val(p,t,i)$ of what it takes to perceive the considered objects o_i soundly and more completely.

Here is the main point of this example: At the phenomenological level alone, without recourse to metaphysics or reductionist epistemology, the phenomenon, the conception (p,t,i) alone yields to reflection an understanding $Val(p,t,i)$ that is highly compelling and essentially dictates what kinds of considerations and observations can and cannot count as leading, if actualized, to further perceptions and observations of "the same thing." That is, the understanding $Val(p,t,i)$ provides at once the constraints on thought and the means to enriching thought necessary to sustain the conviction that, by contemplating o_i, one is contemplating something genuinely objectual.

A phenomenology of error is a theme for another work. But something on the matter has already been said in the Introduction and more can be added. For example, $Val(p,t,i)$ may lead to certain expectations about what sorts of things should be further observable about o_i if it is as prehended in i, if further features adumbrated in i and successive cognitive apprehensions are genuinely there, if o_i is what it seems. Conflict with expectations will typically "explode" (to use a Husserlian word) the prehension or some parts of it and will render the understanding $Val(p,t,i)$ or some parts of it void or irrelevant. Whatever is left of i or $Val(p,t,i)$ will then serve as a foundation for building a new conception (p,t',i'), perhaps having the character of positing in $o_{i'}$ "what was mistakenly taken as o_i."

Example 2. In this example, $p =$ myself, $t =$ the present, $o_i =$ an extended deductive argument I am considering, $i =$ the initial presentation.

I am presented with an extended argument that I hold before me in my mind. The argument is presented to me in the form of a series of connected statements that seems to hang together in a convincing way as a valid argument. I am aware, however, that I do not fully understand all phases of the argument. I do not quite see what certain steps contribute. When I consider the extent to which I grasp the argument and when I look over the phases presented, I become aware of aspects I can and must consider further. For example, I can check whether a key word might have been used in slightly different senses. I can check whether or not a justification for a step in the argument actually agrees with the step taken. I can more closely scrutinize what each statement says and what role it plays in the argument. I can better determine what is taken to be true or what is assumed.

I am mysteriously but clearly aware that such and such a kind of consideration will determine if a word is being used in two different senses. Looking at a step in the argument, I can ask if the claim of A following from B is sound, if the facts about A and B used to justify this claim can always be used to make such an inference, or if one can conceive of a counterexample, thus casting aspersions on the validity of the step.

The very nature of the object o_i (an argument) under the considered conception, its verbal nature in particular, leads one into the argument, produces an understanding of continuously more refined considerations for determining the worth of o_i. Clarifying the use of words (something one needs to know how to do before one can use language), abstracting the properties of statements on which the phases of the argument depend, etc., are all insightfully sustained by the conception (p,t,i) as things to do in order to cognitively apprehend o_i more fully and to determine the argument's validity. The more I brood over the details of the elements in (p,t,i) in the manner indicated, the more an understanding $Val(p,t,i)$ emerges, an understanding of what points to press, what avenues of consideration to follow. This understanding carries with it a fully compelling authority, e.g., there is something strikingly correct and sensible about checking the validity by making sure that at least the key words are being used consistently throughout the argument.

In both of these examples o_i is given in certain respects but not given completely, and this is known; further, inadequately given aspects are adumbrated in the initial apprehensions. In both cases the elements of (p,t,i) seem to frame o_i in such a way that one can read out possible paths through experience and thought that lead to a more complete determination of the object; an understanding $Val(p,t,i)$ accrues. If we consider the compelling, "rational" quality of the elements of such an understanding (e.g., consider the last sentence in the preceding paragraph), then it seems that this understanding in some sense gives us a stable understanding of the object, it seems that $Val(p,t,i)$ fixes the identity of the object, and this is rather miraculous.

In one respect, of course, these phenomenological considerations belabor the obvious. But I think that the very obviousness of such considerations ought to impress us with the following moral: what counts as right and sound thinking about the object is hidden away in, or sustained by the conception of the object. This just means that the grounds on which the objectuality or "reality" of a posited object o_i are ultimately to be decided are to be found in the conception. Any considerations coming from outside the conception, external to the emergent understanding $Val(p,t,i)$ (the last accruing under phenomenological analysis, under analysis of (p,t,i)) will have to do battle with the integrity, with the fully compelling, insightful, "rational" characteristics of the elements composing $Val(p,t,i)$.

I will return to the last matter in III.3. But the crucial issues were already raised in Chapter I: clever logical constructions yielding parsimonious ontologies and psychologistic and physicalistic reductionism may each achieve certain effects in deciding what, for the purposes of such and such a theory of a world, we can ignore, but they can not deny the reality, the actuality, the objectuality of the "eliminated" entities, when a conception (p,t,i) of the entities supports a strong, clear, fully compelling understanding $Val(p,t,i)$. The existence of such an understanding was crucial to our criterion for the existence of abstract objects given in I, and will be used again in III.3.

We must not, however, be too taken by the wonder of finding an understanding $Val(p,t,i)$ to be yielded upon brooding over a phenomenon (p,t,i). Not only is p's understanding fallible relative to his own conception, but also a phenomenon may not make possible or sustain such a stable, strong, invariant $Val(p,t,i)$. The "object" framed by (p,t,i) may be "ill conceived," the conception fraught with hidden confusion and cloaked inconsistency. To the extent that a phenomenon does not sustain such a strong, invariable $Val(p,t,i)$, to that extent the object of the conception o_i will fail to have full cognitive or scientific reality for us. To the extent that the phenomenon is thus unstable, unsolvable problems and irresolvable crises will occur, and the object will increasingly appear to be a phantom object.

I will now give a slightly more extensive example of a case in which an actual scientific crisis was in a certain sense the result of a deeper analysis of $Val(p,t,i)$ than had been achieved previously and of how resolution of the crisis seemed to lie in the direction of a still deeper analysis. I could have taken once again the example from Gödel; I will return to that example later.

Example 3. In the 1840's, the mathematician Karl Weierstrass constructed a function which the finest analysis of the day proved to be continuous, and yet it was also clear that the function was not differentiable.[1] The *geometric intuition* of continuity dictated that all continuous functions are differentiable where defined. Geometric intuition was generally taken to be *the* foundation (*the* source of authority) on which analysis was built. Weierstrass showed that elementary concepts of analysis could be used to construct a function whose existence geometric intuition denies. It could no longer be assumed that mathematical analysis had an adequate foundation in geometric intuition. This led to the attempt to found analysis on the natural numbers and on set theory. Let us consider this example from a phenomenological point of view.

Recalling Example 2, if one does not think to look at certain phases of an argument (e.g., whether a key word is used in different ways), then invalid arguments will seem valid and one will be none the wiser until one "succeeds" in "arguing for" contradictory statements. Then one will have to re-attend to all that is involved in the argument, making an effort to ferret out some unnoticed but crucial part which, once seen, makes clear to one that by ignoring it, one had committed a fallacy. How absurd it seems, once it has been noticed, to use a crucial, pivotal word in different ways throughout an argument. The phenomenon (p,t,i) framed the argument in a way that pointed to, adumbrated, as yet unnoticed properties of the argument which, when a crisis occurred, could be pursued and fully determined. There is a strong parallel here with the case of sense-perception—the phenomenon (p,t,i), for o_i a sense-perceptual object, may frame an object much richer in determinations than are actually presented in acts underlying (p,t,i). So, e.g., (p,t,i) frames a tree, but it frames the tree as having another side, albeit as yet unseen. It may not have explicitly occurred to me

1. J. H. Manheim, *The Genesis of Point Set Topology* (London, 1964).

that I take the tree as having another side, although brooding over (p,t,i) reveals that the tree is framed in precisely this way. It may likewise not have occurred to me that I could obtain a more complete perception of the tree by looking at the other side, but this possibility is supported by the content of the conception, presenting or framing as it does something "with another side." This possibility for achieving a more complete perception of the tree (an understanding of this possibility is a part of $Val(p,t,i)$) was framed or adumbrated in the phenomenon, the conception (p,t,i) and, just as I have done, could be brought out by achieving greater self-consciousness with regard to the elements of the conception (i.e., by phenomenological reflection).

Return now to the case of Weierstrass' function. The relevant (p,t,i) framed a world of mathematical objectivities pointing to entities with properties outside the scope of geometric intuition. But because of a too shallow awareness of all that was so framed in the relevant phenomena (p,t,i), e.g., all of the conceptual possibilities and possibilities for conceptual construction and proof latently framed, no one suspected that such things as Weierstrass' function were to be found within the domain of mathematical analysis. No one was motivated to go more critically through the contents of the relevant (p,t,i), evaluating the worth of the understanding $Val(p,t,i)$ giving primacy to geometric intuition (but not necessarily to the understanding most fully supported by the underlying conception). But the way in which the revelant (p,t,i) framed the world of mathematical analysis allowed Weierstrass to construct the geometrically recalcitrant function in a perfectly compelling way, thereby forcing a much deeper contemplation of the phenomenon, pressing for a corrected understanding $Val(p,t,i)$ of what kind of consideration and *Evidenz* must be taken as foundational for analysis. What was called for, in short, was penetrating phenomenological analysis, an analysis of the relevant (p,t,i) pushed further than ever before.

III.2. Phenomenological Ontology

A phenomenon (p,t,i) frames the objectivity o_i, not only in the sense of containing all that p has (during t) on which to build his knowledge and thus all that is regulative of what counts as knowledge of o_i, but also in the sense of sustaining an increasingly refinable understanding $Val(p,t,i)$ of what further thoughts and experiences could, if actualized in the stream of p's conscious life, answer questions about o_i, yielding further experiences and knowledge of o_i.

The aspects of consciousness (aspects of (p,t,i) in particular) that so frame an object or domain of objects, o_i, are regarded by Husserl as "implicit systems of intentionality." It is one purpose of transcendental phenomenology to make those systems, those framing effects of (p,t,i) explicit. Why? We have already seen in the Introduction, II, and III.1, how our knowledge-building depends on clarifying what frames the object o_i of cognitive pursuit; such clarification is important lest we end up with a theory concerned with some other object (albeit perhaps without our noticing this) because we did not attend to all that was demanded of us by (p,t,i) and, most especially, by the most strongly supported $Val(p,t,i)$. Another principal application of phenomenology, which is, however, at root a variation of the last-mentioned, is that of settling problems of ontology.

An ultimate goal of transcendental phenomenology is the complete clarification of the logos of all conceivable being,[2] to determine all possible *Seinsinne*, all possible conceptions

2. Edmund Husserl, *Cartesian Meditations*, trans. D. Cairns (The Hague, 1960), p. 155.

of being. The reason? "All wrong interpretations of being come from naive blindness to the horizons that join together in determining the *Seinsinn,* and to the corresponding task of uncovering implicit intentionality." [3] What is accomplished by the analysis of *Seinsinne?* As Husserl said, correcting all wrong interpretations of being, and this seems to mean determining the limits of the validity of being- and truth-ascriptions. Two major examples of the use of *Seinsinn*-analysis correcting such misinterpretations are to be found in Husserl's writings: his showing that the *Ding-an-sich* interpretation is wrong for the world that is the object of the natural attitude,[4] and his correction of the solipsistic "transcendental illusion," viz., "if everything I accept as existent (e.g., the world there for everyone) is constituted in my own ego [i.e., is framed by my own conceptions], then everything existent depends on my transcendental being [the field of one's own subjectivity]." [5] One corrects these wrong interpretations, one performs the *Sinn*-analysis, not by the analysis of the meaning of words (it is not a linguistic *Sinn* at issue), but by the analysis of the relevant phenomena, by what Husserl speaks of as "the intentionalities, syntheses, and motivations" in which the considered objectualities o_i become "constituted," that is, by the analyses of the relevant conceptions (p,t,i) wherein the objectualities become framed in initial prehensions and further cognition regulated under the foundational, increasingly improved understanding Val (p,t,i).

In our ongoing cognitive activities (e.g., physics, mathematics, theology), we pursue objects without a perfectly

---

3. Ibid., p. 85.

4. Edmund Husserl, *Ideas,* trans. W. R. B. Gibson (New York, 1969), para. 48, 52.

5. Edmund Husserl, *Formal and Transcendental Logic,* trans. D. Cairns (The Hague, 1969), p. 241; *Ideas,* para. 55; *Cartesian Meditations,* Fifth Meditation.

clear sense of their nature as objects and of the limits of validity of certain modes of thought in dealing with them. We typically proceed on the foundation of a naive feeling that we are doing the right thing, pursuing the objects in a valid way. There is a tendency, however, to let certain a priori constructions of being intrude, either through metaphysical convictions (e.g., physicalism, sensationalism, idealism) or through uncritical applications of logical principles (e.g., not only convictions about logical laws being valid, such as the law of the excluded middle, but also convictions about what count as logically clear or precise statements, statements of possible cognitive worth). Such a priori constructions may radically exclude the possibility of entering a cognitive domain, as the application of physicalism may exclude theology or the full aesthetic world, as the application of classical objectual reasoning may exclude hope of access to the world of intuitionistic mathematics (and as application of intuitionistic principles may make impossible access to the world of classical mathematics), and as certain kinds of stringent principles of what count as logically sound and significant statements may perhaps wrongly preclude one from making aesthetic or ethical judgments in an objective and objectively significant manner, while such judgments may be possible under other, but nevertheless sound, principles.

The analysis of *Seinsinne* determines, then, the way in which considered entities naively cognitively pursued may be considered objective or objectual, viz., how they must be thought about, under what principles of validation and clarity, if they are to be thought about rightly and fruitfully. Thus, one could ask:

In what way is intersubjective Nature objectual?
In what was is a number objectual?
In what way is the physical world objectual?
In what way is a sound objectual?

In what way is a quark objectual?

In what way is "the supernatural world" objectual?

In what way is the world of nonassociative algebras objectual?

In what way is the meaning of words objectual?

In what ways are prices, poems, God, . . . objectual?

What counts as an adequate response to 'In what way . . . ?'?

Let us consider Husserl's solution to the problem of explicating the *Seinsinn* "*x* truly is" for specific *x*'s (e.g., world objects in worlds). What should such an explication look like? The being of an object is determined for Husserl by "the horizons [of implicit intentionality] which join together in determining [how an object *is*]." What could count as giving us an adequate explication? In '*x* truly is if, and only if, . . . ', what should we put in the place of the ' . . . '?

It is a principal thesis of Husserl's, a thesis not without immediate intuitive appeal and considerable cogency (at least of the order of Peirce's Pragmatic Maxim), that nothing can have "reality" for us save that it is given to us in some adequate way, save that it is experienceable in the broadest sense of 'experience'—given to us in an act of consciousness. Insofar as an object "touches" our consciousness, to that extent, and only to that extent, will it have reality for us. Of course, *this* can be made clear only by giving a theory of all possible "acts of consciousness" and, in a way, such theories are what transcendental phenomenology is principally concerned with.

The hypothetical assumption of a Real Something outside this world is indeed a "logically" possible one, and there is clearly no formal contradiction in making it. But if we question the essential conditions of its validity, the kind of evidence (*Ausweisung*) demanded by its very meaning and the nature of the evidential generally as determined in principle through the thesis of a transcendent . . . we perceive that the transcendent must needs be *experienceable,* and not merely by an Ego conjured into being as an empty logical possibility but by any *actual* Ego, as the demonstrable (*ausweisbare*) unity of its systematic experience.[6]

And,

Everything that we call by the name of *Object,* that of which we speak, what we see before us as reality, hold to be possible or probable, think of in however vague a way, is insofar already an object of consciousness; and this means that whatever the world and reality may be or be called must be represented within the limits of real and possible consciousness by corresponding meanings and positions, filled more or less with intuitional content.[7]

Also,

"The real world", as it is called, the correlate of our factual experience, then presents itself as a special case of various possible worlds and non-worlds, which, on their side, are no other than correlates of the essentially possible variations of the idea "empirical consciousness." [8]

Husserl extracts the essence of these compelling insights and places them in a central thesis, the Thesis of Reason, the *Vernunftthesis,* which occurs throughout his writings in various forms. I will present two versions, of which the second is officially called "the Thesis of Reason":

To every region and category of would-be objects [e.g., objective domains, worlds] corresponds phenomenologically not only a basic kind of meaning or position, but also a basic . . . type of primordial *Evidenz.*[9]

Categories of *Evidenz* and objectuality are correlates of one another.[10]

And, the *Vernunftthesis:*

6. Husserl, *Ideas,* para. 48.   7. Ibid., para. 135.
8. Ibid., para. 47.   9. Ibid., para. 38.
10. Husserl, *Formal and Transcendental Logic,* para. 60.

To every object "that truly is" there intrinsically corresponds the idea of a possible consciousness in which the object itself can be grasped in an originary and perfectly adequate way. Conversely, when this possibility is guaranteed, the object is "that which truly is." [11]

In brief, by Husserl's analyses, we are justified in asserting that 'x truly is' if and only if we can find intrinsically corresponding to x a category of possible *Evidenz*, a category of adequate acts of consciousness, capable of presenting x with increasing completeness. That is, x can have "reality" for us (perhaps one should add "cognitive reality") only insofar as x is being adequately presented and insofar as we can clearly see how we might continue to experience more completely and to think about x.

The intrinsic correspondence between x and a category of *Evidenz* is, of course, a correspondence provided on the foundation of the relevant phenomena. From my point of view, the correspondence is presented on the foundation of the understanding $Val(p,t,i)$. The richness and coherence of this understanding will give us the feeling or sense that we are indeed directing our attention, when directing our attention to o_i, to something "real," to something nonillusory.

It is interesting that Carnap comes to *vaguely* similar conclusions when he writes "to accept the thing-world means nothing more than to accept a certain form of language, in other words, to accept rules for forming statements *and for testing, accepting, or rejecting them*" [my emphasis].[12] Of course, in pointing to $Val(p,t,i)$ as the source of "rules for testing, accepting, or rejecting" assertions about a world, we have a hope of tying together our inner conception of a world

11. Husserl, *Ideas,* para. 142.

12. Rudolf Carnap, "Empiricism, Semantics, and Ontology," in *Philosophy of Mathematics,* ed. P. Benacerraf and H. Putnam (Englewood Cliffs, N.J., 1964).

(the world as framed by (p,t,i) and, in particular, the elements in our experience and thought which inspire us to cognitively pursue a world) and the relevant category of *Evidenz*. In the phenomenon, in "the underlying systems of intentionalities," inspiring, say, a physicist's or Paracelsus' conception of "the real world," there must be a coherent and sound understanding $Val(p,t,i)$ if, in the long run, the object of that conception, the purported world, is to continue to have "reality" for p.

Phenomenological ontology is concerned with an explication of all possible forms of "the real," and, by the considerations above, this means that phenomenological ontology is concerned with all possible sound and coherent $Val(p,t,i)$ establishing or making manifest "an intrinsic correspondence" between o_i and forms of *Evidenz*, of adequate acts of consciousness, founding cognition and thought about o_i.

III.3. A Cognitively Contentual Criterion for the Existence of Objective Domains (Worlds)

In the previous sections the thesis emerged that, if o_i is to have cognitive reality for us, then (p,t,i) must found a sufficiently sound understanding $Val(p,t,i)$ of which experiences and thoughts (mental states, acts) may be rightly used in building and justifying theories of o_i. If o_i is an objective domain and if it is to be an object of successful scientific study, the relevant phenomenon must possess a relatively stable "nucleus" framing o_i and capable of being apprehended by p, yielding an increasingly improved understanding $Val(p,t,i)$ of which experiences and thoughts may be used in constructing justifiable theories of o_i. Otherwise, p would have *no* foundation other than arbitrary convention or speculation on which to build a justifiable theory of o_i. If there

were no such compelling understanding *Val* closely motivated and sustained throughout by (p,t,i) (in the sense of
III.1) then p could make arbitrary choices and so have o_i be
whatever he willed or desired it to be. But then there can be
no genuine object of and for thought, for such thought is
unconstrained, and so anything can be thought of its "object."

The considerations of III.1 and III.2 lead us to a fruitful
attitude toward the problem of the cognitive content of questions of the existence of objective domains and isolate the
nucleus of intellectual experience making the Husserlian
criterion useful and plausible.

Let us examine the Husserlian theses about the "true
being" of entities with a view to simplifying the argument
and resulting criterion for "real being," "true being."

Scientific inquiry begins when p's cognitive interest is
aroused by the disclosure or presentation of an apparent
objective domain. The domain may be poorly presented, as
the physical-mechanical world was presented to Newton at
the beginning of his researches, or as the domain of set theory
was presented to Cantor when he first began to appreciate
the significance of treating, e.g., infinite sets, orders of infinity, derived sets.[13] In such cases, the relevant phenomena
(p,t,i), o_i an objective domain, are poorly apprehended. If a
science of the domain is possible, however, then elements in
the phenomena framing o_i should be sufficiently accessible
and determinate to suggest lines of inquiry capable of being
fruitfully pursued on the foundation of increasingly improved
justification, with increasingly stronger justifying grounds,
to the point of full satisfaction of cognitive interest. (See
III.1, Examples 1–3, for illustrations of what I mean.)

13. J. W. Dauben, "The Trigonometric Background to Georg Cantor's Theory of Sets," *Archive for the History of Exact Science,* 7 (1971),
181–216.

Suppose that for p there is a conception, phenomenon, (p,t,i) whose elements yield such fruitful and promising lines of inquiry and observation, which p is pursuing, producing rich, intriguing theory, sustained by increasingly powerful and clear justification. Any argument (e.g., reductionist, metaphysical, physicalist, psychologistic) to the effect that o_i as characterized in the emergent theory does not exist would be in total conflict with the integrity of the presentation of o_i, with the richness and justifying power of the $Val(p,t,i)$ sustained by the underlying phenomenon. Unless it could be shown that any attempt to produce a sound and adequate, justified theory of o_i leads to an imbroglio of conceptual confusions, contradictions, and other such theoretical aporias, any purported argument against the existence of o_i would seem to p *not* to be an argument about o_i, or, at best, would seem a hunch about the still undisclosed fate of p's study of o_i. An argument could concern o_i only if its right to have an effect were guaranteed by $Val(p,t,i)$, for otherwise the argument, not founded on what frames the identity of o_i, would not touch o_i save in a weakly analogical or even metaphorical way. It is hard to imagine what a strong nonexistence proof for the apparent object o_i would be like if it were not ultimately based upon some insight into the basic coherence of any $Val(p,t,i)$ sustained by (p,t,i). Suppose that the argument depended on some "metaphysical claim" such as "only physical objects exist," "there are no subjective states, only behavior," or "we can know only our own ideas." Then in view of his cognitive and scientific successes with o_i and the promise of more such successes (because of the richness of Val and the clarity, certainty, and authority of the justifying powers it provides), p would probably think himself irrational if he did not regard this success as disproof of those claims, as casting aspersions on the *Evidenz* giving them authority, or at least as reason for objecting to them and for not otherwise letting them impede his work. Let us then propose:

Thesis of the existence of objective domains: p is justified in asserting the existence of an objective domain o_i when, on the basis of p's understanding $Val(p,t,i)$, p can successfully construct increasingly sound, justifiable theory of o_i.

p would not be justified in asserting the nonexistence of a purported objective domain simply because the conditions of the thesis were not met. A complete breakdown of progress in research, hopeless inconsistencies, and conceptual confusions may simply reflect on the quality of p's powers to penetrate the relevant phenomenon, on the quality of p's intellectual resources. Although the thesis does not illuminate the question of the nonexistence of objective domains, it does shed light on or explain the cognitive content of questions about their existence; it explains when p is justified in asserting the existence of objective domains. Precisely because phenomena form genuine objects of thought (by the criterion for the existence of abstract objects in Chapter I), as has been pointed out in Chapter II, and because reflection on a phenomenon (p,t,i) yields an understanding $Val(p,t,i)$, we may rightfully regard this criterion for the existence of objective domains as genuinely "cognitively contentual."

The achievement and explication of an understanding $Val(p,t,i)$ may be loosely described as providing "a phenomenological ontology for o_i." 'Ontology' is used because such an analysis decides the "objective" or "scientific" *reality* of o_i for p (i.e., whether or not p is justified in asserting the existence of o_i). 'Phenomenology' is used because an understanding $Val(p,t,i)$ is motivated throughout and sustained by a phenomenon (p,t,i).

Many themes are connected with phenomenological ontology that can and must be pursued in considerable detail. Perhaps the most pressing is the problem of "transcendental intersubjectivity," the problem of determining on what grounds different p's may be said to have access to the same world o_i, if their access and openness to o_i ultimately goes back to a phenomenon (p,t,i). Husserl has done much to clarify this problem and to show us the way to its solution,[14] but more work is needed here. In some sense, solving this last problem is of secondary importance, for whatever has "scientific reality" for me on the basis of a clear, certain understanding $Val(p,t,i)$ cannot be stolen from me by deficiencies in others, e.g., their lack of sufficient background in thought and experience. I do not mean to treat the matter frivolously, but only to point out that in some deep and strong sense it is ultimately that which I can see clearly and with insightful certainty that I "rationally" accept, however the rest of the world drifts; self-responsibility must come before shared experience and shared cognitive interest, providing the foundation for the latter.

To conclude this chapter, I will briefly discuss two areas in which careful phenomenological research into the structure of $Val(p,t,i)$, particularly concrete and highly specialized research, promises to shed light on some matters of current interest.

(1) *The Problem of Platonism in Mathematics.* I have already discussed, albeit sketchily, Gödel's mathematical Platonism and the respects in which phenomenologically more refined analyses might clarify this. I will now discuss the matter further, without claiming in any sense to offer a definitive account; it would go beyond the scope of the present work to include all that needs to be considered.

Gödel has written:

14. Husserl, *Cartesian Meditations,* Fifth Meditation.

But, despite their [the sets'] remoteness from sense experience, we do have something like a perception also of the objects of set theory, as is seen from the fact that the axioms force themselves upon us as being true. I don't see any reason why we should have less confidence in this kind of perception, i.e., in mathematical intuition, than in sense perception, which induces us to build up physical theories and to expect that future sense perceptions will agree with them.[15]

Although Gödel did not theoretically clarify what he meant by the "mathematical intuition" or mode of "perception" underlying set theory, he did give cogent and concrete examples of kinds of considerations that can, without the intrusion of elements of arbitrariness, decide compellingly, insightfully, and rationally questions in set theory independent of the usual axioms. (The reader should recall the discussion in the Introduction.) Gödel's treatment shows to some extent that there exists a sufficiently rich and cogent $Val(p,t,i)$ sustained by the prehension i (as discussed in the Introduction). By our criterion for the existence of objective domains, objective realities, the existence of such a $Val(p,t,i)$ is sufficient ground for asserting the existence of such an o_i. The existence of such a $Val(p,t,i)$ does not *prove* that the domain of set theory, o_i, exists. But the continued emergence of possible considerations, considerations compellingly sustained by $Val(p,t,i)$, considerations which, if carried through, could decide questions about o_i without arbitrariness and with compelling cogency, is reason for taking seriously the claim that o_i has objective reality. If there is finally a breakdown in which it becomes clear that set-theoretical "knowledge" could be completed only on the foundation of arbitrary choices and ad hoc considerations, then we may rightly doubt that o_i is a well-determined objective reality. (Notice that in the ar-

15. Kurt Gödel, Appendix to "What Is Cantor's Continuum Problem?" in *Philosophy of Mathematics,* ed. P. Benacerraf and H. Putnam.

ticle cited in note 15 Gödel takes pains to point out that a distinction must be made between the objective cogency of our set-theoretic thinking and the full logical, foundational reconstruction and clarification of that thinking; the last is still a problem, for previous efforts have led to antinomies and, from certain points of view, ad hoc devices for avoiding the antinomies.)

In reference to the quotation from Gödel above, Chihara writes: "But even if we grant that there are such 'mathematical experiences,' must we assume that the mathematical theories we construct in response to these experiences are true? Must we assume that the axioms of set theory are true in order to explain our mathematical intuitions? I can find no convincing reasons for thinking we must." [16] I think that the Criterion for the Existence of Objective Domains provides the solution to Chihara's dilemma. The existence of a strong $Val(p,t,i)$ assures us that we will not be disappointed in taking to be the case what seems to be the case (in taking things as they appear, in taking things phenomenologically), viz., that in thinking about o_i we are directing our attention to something objectively real.

The psychologically and phenomenologically important point is that so positing o_i as a well-determined objective reality is by no means an *"als ob,"* as if, postulation. It is not a convenient fiction. Exactly as in the case of sense-perception (the reader is referred back to Chapter I for the analogy of various forms of observation with sense-perceptual observation, the analogy which gives 'exactly' here its sense and authority), when we direct or seem to direct our thoughts to

16. Charles S. Chihara, *Ontology and the Vicious Circle Principle* (Ithaca, N.Y., 1973), p. 77. For another critique of Gödel's Platonism which is in conflict with the phenomenological (e.g., it requires "external," physical or metaphysical, connections between knower and known), see Paul Benacerraf, "Mathematical Truth," *Journal of Philosophy*, 70 (1972), 661–679.

the domain of set theory (1) we find our thoughts constrained, and (2) we find paths of considerations that rationally, insightfully, compellingly enrich our thoughts, giving our emergent thoughts the character of being true thoughts of the same domain, the domain of set theory. If there is an element of "as if" here at all, it occurs when we cognitively pursue but have not completely apprehended any seeming "objective reality."

(2) *The Problem of Stable Designation.* Perhaps *the* central issue in the philosophy of science is that of making clear how we can have a succession of increasingly improved theories of "the same thing," the same objective domain. For a discussion of these matters and a survey of current work, the reader is referred elsewhere.[17] One important part of the problem may be thought of (albeit rather too simply) in the following manner. If our current theory of o_i embodies what we are currently willing to call our best understanding of o_i, what grounds outside of the theory do we have upon which to improve our theory? Our phenomenological studies suggest that a study of the relevant $Val(p,t,i)$ would or could yield at least a partial solution to this problem. On the foundation of an initial prehension i of o_i and, in particular, on the foundation of continuously pursued and illuminated adumbrations in i of further, apprehensible aspects of o_i, an understanding, an increasingly strong and compelling understanding $Val(p,t,i)$ emerges of what kinds of considerations and observations will decide questions about o_i. $Val(p,t,i)$ ultimately stabilizes our theoretical thinking about o_i (at least insofar as o_i has scientific, objective, reality for us); it shows us that such and such closer, theory-correcting observations lead to better apprehension of "the same thing," o_i. It

17. For summaries, critiques, and references, see, e.g., Arthur Fine, "How to Compare Theories: Reference and Change," *Nous*, 9 (1975), 17-32; also Israel Scheffler, *Science and Subjectivity* (New York, 1967).

gives us the *reasons* for changing theories, and thus simultaneously provides for the identity of the intended object of thought. Husserl's work *Crisis of the European Sciences and Transcendental Phenomenology* may be construed as presenting us with a beginning of the essential phenomenological analyses; the important thing is to learn to choose the important i for, say, physics. Husserl may be construed as arguing that such an appropriate i could be any "perception-of-things-in-the-*Lebenswelt*." I think this is a promising line. (The Appendix presents some of Husserl's insights into what I construe as the stabilizing effects of $Val(p,t,i)$.)

IV | Logic

The principal contribution Chapter IV makes to the foundations of logic is to show, on the basis of phenomenological ontology (in the sense discussed in Chapter III), that there exist different worlds or objective domains W and V such that, for the purposes of formulating true and adequate theories of these domains, W and V require different logics. In particular, it will be argued that a world exists requiring classical logic and that another world exists requiring intuitionistic logic. Following out ideas of Charles Parsons,[1] one could also show that a world or objective domain exists requiring substitutional quantification theory. Of course, the objective domains considered are by no means the only domains requiring the considered logics. The main point is to establish that there are different domains requiring different logics.

This contribution is not altogether trivial for five reasons. First, there are still many people who have apotheosized classical, objectual quantification theory, regarding it as "the universal logic." If, however, there exist objective domains which require a nonclassical logic, then this entails that one can not take up validity or appropriateness of classical rea-

1. Charles Parsons, "A Plea for Substitutional Quantification Theory," *Journal of Philosophy*, 68 (1971), 231–238; "Ontology and Mathematics," *Philosophical Review*, 80 (1972), 151–176.

soning for granted; for every objective domain one must reach a rational decision about the valid or appropriate logic. Choosing a logic—save for hardly practicable pragmatic rules of thumb—is a problem for which the history of logic and logic theory has not, I think, altogether prepared us. Second, if there exists a domain W requiring a nonclassical logic, then, of course, one can not assume, as e.g., W. V. Quine has assumed,[2] that one can always contrive to use only classical logic. I will argue that there is such a domain. In particular, one cannot contrive to have an adequate, complete theory of W. Third, if one can recognize that a domain W requires a logic L and that another domain V requires a logic M, L different from M, then this shows that "our conceptual apparatus" [3] is not too strongly regulated by one logic. Fourth, if there are different logics appropriate for different worlds, then our naive understanding of logic truths" as assertions "true in all possible worlds" is wrong. This implies that there are different concepts of truth which different logics may be interpreted as embodying. Thus, the notions "logical truth" and "truth" lose some of their unequivocalness and aprioricity. Fifth, the means we use to show that there are different worlds requiring different logics, phenomenological means, establish connections between formal and informal reasoning, the latter motivating and regulating the former (see IV.2); that is, there is the promise that a full theory of all possible $Val(p,t,i)$ will yield a theory of the connections between informal and formal logic. Since the connection we do find is *nonempirical*, and thus not susceptible to regulation by positivistic criteria, one might hope that a full theory of all possible $Val(p,t,i)$ would yield the means to carry out perfectly clarified "transcendental deductions" of the appropri-

2. W. V. Quine, *Philosophy of Logic* (Englewood Cliffs, N.J., 1970), chap. 6.
3. Quine, *Methods of Logic*, rev. ed. (New York, 1961).

ateness of considered logics for considered objective domains, making it completely clear that logic is not an empirical but rather a "transcendental" subject. Before this hope can be taken seriously, however, considerable phenomenological and logical groundwork must be done. What I have tried to do is to relate phenomenology and logic, showing that there is, in phenomena and the corresponding *Val*'s, a nonempirical connection between logics and worlds. Just how strong this connection is remains for further work to discover. The important task for now is to make plausible that such a connection exists and to bring out some of the considerations, both logical and phenomenological, that will have to be made in order to achieve full clarity.

IV.1 establishes the existence of domains requiring different logics. IV.2 locates some of the "logic-free" aspects of our thought, characterizing some of the nature of informal reasoning. IV.3 discusses the problem of dealing with equivocations in the notion "truth" forced upon our attention by IV.1.

IV.1. On the Existence of Different Objective Domains Requiring Different Logics

In this section I will consider two objective domains (worlds). One can argue, on the basis of the criterion given in Chapter III for justifiably asserting the existence of purportedly existing worlds, that the considered domains exist. The point of these examples is to show that here are distinct domains requiring logics for the purposes of formulating true and adequate theories of the domains, for rightly reasoning about the domains, and also for showing the bearing of phenomenological analysis on the matter. I will make no pretense of considering these examples in full. That would require a much more extensive presentation than I have made. The point is to clarify the bearing of phenomenological reflection on the problem of deciding among logics. For the reasons given above, this is not something altogether insignificant.

In the first example, o_i is the domain of extensive, geometric continua. In the second example, o_i is "the physical, fully objective world." In the first example it happens that a series of phenomenological analyses leads to a mathematical analysis of geometric continua carrying with it the implication that a nonclassical, and presumably constructive, logic is required. In the second example, the need for classical logic makes itself felt in an entirely different way—one uses classical, objectual logic in advance in order to constitute, in order to achieve access to, perfectly objectual physical nature. The difference, however, is not really as great as it may seem, for in the first case, the choice of mathematics that forces a constructive logic is made in order to keep and have present precisely the world of qualitatively extensive geometric continua.

Example 1. $o_i =$ the domain of qualitatively extensive geometric continua.

This example is taken from Hermann Weyl, and the reader is referred to him for a sense of historical context.[4]

Point-set theory, especially point-set topology, provides a powerful theory of mathematical continua, which, although it leaves many questions undecided, provides a successful foundation for real analysis and its natural generalizations. There is, however, a conflict of sorts between geometric intuition and point-set continua. Counterintuitive constructions can be made on the foundation of the claim that talk of point-set continua forms an adequate theory of geometric

4. Hermann Weyl, *Philosophy of Mathematics and Natural Science* (New York, 1963), chap. 2, sec. 9.

(intuitive, qualitative) continua. I will point out some considerations suggesting that geometric continua have a mathematical content which is not fully captured, or is misleadingly analyzed, by point-set continua. I will first discuss a counterintuitive construction made possible by the "reduction" of geometric continua to point-set continua. Next I will argue that in fact the reduction has more a hypothetical and conjectural air about it than that of a genuine, hardnosed mathematical reduction. Finally, I will explain how Hermann Weyl's attempt to capture more adequately the mathematical content of geometric continua forces a nonclassical logic. The reader should observe that I do not, as Weyl seems to do, consider the theory of point-set continua as false or absurd. Given the criterion for the existence of objective domains in Chapter III, I must admit that the domain of point-set continua exists. What I am questioning is whether or not one rightfully supposes that the mathematical content of geometric continua is adequately captured or framed in point-set terms. More precisely, what I am doing here is arguing principally that there exists a domain of qualitative geometric continua that has a mathematical content not captured by construing the domain set-theoretically.

The example of a geometrically counterintuitive point-set construction is the one called 'the Banach-Tarski Paradox'.[5] By means of free-group constructions, one can show that any sphere can be decomposed into a finite number of disjoint parts that can be reassembled as two spheres congruent both to each other and to the original sphere. This certainly flies in the face of geometric intuition, in the sense that any effort to imagine drawing lines on the surface of the sphere having the property such that you could cut the sphere on those lines and reassemble it as two spheres equal to the first will produce the strong conviction that this is impossible. It seems impossible because one thinks of the sphere as qualitatively extensive and rigid. If, however, one thinks of the sphere as a set of points, then one can readily make plausible to oneself the possibility of such a construction. Let me give an example of a consideration that makes the possibility of such a construction plausible, even though the construction itself does not have the properties of the Banach-Tarski construction and furthermore cannot be carried out (but, in an odd way, the intuition is almost the right one): take a sphere qua set of points; now take "every other point"; separate the two "spheres"; they are congruent to each other and to the original. From the point of view of extensive, qualitative geometric continua, such constructions are irrelevant and depend upon something not qualitatively extensive, viz., sets of widthless, dimensionless, points.

G. H. Hardy emphatically made a distinction between "the arithmetic continuum" and the "geometric continuum." In doing so he emphasized that in mathematical analysis the geometric continuum plays a subsidiary role: "The aggregate of all real numbers, rational and irrational, is called the *arithmetic continuum*. It is convenient to suppose that the straight line . . . is composed of points corresponding to all of the numbers of the arithmetical continuum, and of no others." Of this matter of convenience Hardy remarks: "This supposition is merely a hypothesis adopted (i) because it suffices for the purposes of our geometry and (ii) because it provides us with a convenient illustration of analytical process." [6] Of course, Hardy is, among other things, making the point that mathematical analysis may in principle be done

6. G. H. Hardy, *A Course of Pure Mathematics*, 10th ed. (Cambridge, Eng., 1958), p. 24. See also Dauben, "The Trigonometric Background to Georg Cantor's Theory of Sets," p. 207, for Cantor's attitude.

without reference to geometric intuition. But his making this point reminds us that there is room for our having allowed our geometric intuitions to be corrupted by the heuristic value of having an intuitive representation of analytical results.

There is no theorem in analysis entailing that the linear continuum of our geometric intuition is *composed of points*. Consider how one justifies the supposition that the linear geometric continuum is an aggregate of points. One supposes that two distinct points have been "placed" on the linear continuum. Then, using the line segment (as determined by the points) as a unit, one shows how all the rational numbers may be "placed" on the continuum in a way that preserves their natural ordering. Every convergent sequence of rational numbers is then construed as "placing" on the continuum the real number to which it converges. Furthermore, given any "point" on the geometric continuum, one shows how to construct a sequence of rationals converging to "it."

It is important to note that, in the explanation above, I spoke of "placing" the numbers on the geometric continuum. This is all we can claim to have done—to have overlaid the geometric continuum with the real numbers. One has no right to claim that the geometric continuum consists of points (corresponding to the real numbers) simply because one has visualized this overlay. In fact, there is a tradition of convincing intuition that cannot conceive the continuum of geometric intuition to be composed of points.[7] For example, it is difficult to see how something spatially continuous could be composed of discrete, discontinuous, and widthless entities. A geometric continuum is spatial in character, it is extensive, and thus it has a qualitative dimension which is not in the least captured by a set of points with a linear, uncountably dense ordering. That is, the relation between ele-

7. Weyl, *Philosophy of Mathematics,* chap. 2, sec. 9.

ment and set does not seem to be appropriate for building up an analysis of the geometric continuum, however important its role in analyzing the arithmetic continuum.

The notion of a point as an entity whose only discernable property is that it stands in a certain ordering with other points seems, thus put, to verge on the nonsensical. If one permits abstraction from the qualitative aspects of extensive continua or, what are the same things, geometric continua, one is left with the suggestion that perhaps these "points" are only conceptual contrivances serving as placeholders in the geometric world for real numbers. Perhaps it would be better to talk of real numbers or "placed" real numbers, and talk no more of an *extensive* or geometric continuum composed of points.

Now consider the following criticism. Someone might say, I agree that there is a geometric intuition of an extensive continuum where the idea of such things being composed entirely of discrete, widthless points is absurd or very difficult (even if the concept of points—even widthless geometric points—is not). But isn't this intuition simply something superfluous and misleading, a vestige of the historical origins of our concept of the continuum? Continua are really point-sets.

The reply is, I do not deny that there are point-set "continua" and that, indeed, such continua are precisely analyzed in terms of the arithmetic continuum, and vice versa. Point-set theory has its phenomenological ontology; there is a sufficiently rich and constrained understanding Val underlying it. Also, the relevant phenomena (p,t,i), $o_i =$ extensive geometric continua, as I have so far explained, have enough content, a deep enough unity, to provide a $Val(p,t,i)$ capable of leading to and sustaining a full and rich mathematics of a rather different character from point-set theory.

Note that we have already suggested that the relation of

set-theoretic elementhood is not going to be adequate as the basic logical relation for constructing a mathematics of extensive continua. This already makes it clear that it would be surprising if classical logic were appropriate. It will be of further interest to see whether or not the concept of truth embodied by the logic required by the domain of extensive continua will support the law of the excluded middle.

Hermann Weyl and L. E. J. Brouwer provide us with the mathematics needed for the considered domain, the domain of extensive continua; of course, the choice of mathematics is inspired and regulated by the relevant *Val.* (N.B., it may turn out that a more profound analysis of the relevant phenomenon will reveal that this mathematics is inadequate, as a phenomenological analysis given along the lines suggested above—for I have not given a complete phenomenological analysis—would reveal that a point-set analysis was incorrect.)

Weyl suggested that geometric continua be analyzed as follows:

The continuum falls under the notion of the 'extensive whole', which Husserl characterizes as that "which permits a dismemberment of such a kind that the pieces are by their very nature of the same lowest species as is determined by the undivided whole". The division scheme of the one-dimensional continuum is best illustrated by the example of a finite line segment. By halving it, one decomposes it into two parts, a left (10) and a right one (11); each of the latter, by again halving them, decomposes into a left and right one, 100, 101, and 110, 111 respectively, and so on.[8]

Each indefinitely continued binary string
$$b = b_1 b_2 \ldots b_k b_{k+1} \ldots ,$$
where $b_n = 0$ or 1, determines a nesting of extensive parts of the finite line segment, where $b_1 b_2 \ldots b_k b_{k+1}$ is a proper extension of $b_1 b_2 \ldots b_k$.

If we allowed such sequences to go on to infinity or in any

8. Ibid., p. 53.

way assumed that they did, we would in effect be construing the extensive continuum as the discrete point-set continuum. To allow this is to fail to analyze the extensive continuum. If one goes too far, the quality of extensiveness is lost. It is here, I think, that Brouwer's constructive methods become useful, for they provide us with a means of building a mathematics of extensive continua under the restriction that none of the binary strings are actually infinite.

Let B be a set of methods admitted for constructing such binary strings, methods that allow their indefinite continuation, but that never presuppose any such binary strings to be actually infinite.

Call 'an analysis of I' (I is the considered extensive line segment) a property R for which it can be proved by constructive methods (at least methods not presupposing an actual infinite) that

for any indefinitely continued string b generated by methods B we can find a k such that b restricted to $b_1 \ldots b_k$ has the property R.

In symbols, $\forall b \exists k R[b_1 \ldots b_k]$. For the general case in which we have a potentially infinite set of numerals available and in which strings may be constructed according to B by using any of the numerals, Brouwer "proved" a theorem ("the bar theorem") to the effect that, for the truth of $\forall b \exists k R[b_1 \ldots b_k]$, it is necessary and sufficient to justify a certain principle of inductive definition over B relative to R. This theorem is true classically, but one necessarily assumes that the b's are infinite. (In the case where the number of numerals is finite, the theorem is classically equivalent to König's infinity lemma.[9]) Brouwer has given a constructive (albeit controversial [10]) "proof" of this theorem. In the case

9. S. C. Kleene and R. E. Vesley, *The Foundations of Intuitionistic Mathematics* (Amsterdam, 1965), pp. 52, 53, and 59.

10. E.g., Charles Parsons, "Comments," in *From Frege to Gödel*, ed. J. van Heijenoort (Cambridge, Mass., 1967), pp. 447–453.

where b_n can only be 0 or 1 (the case we are interested in), the theorem has the following constructive consequence:

there is a natural number N such that

$\forall b R[b_1 \ldots b_n]$.

This in turn has the powerful consequence that all functions defined on B into B relative to the analysis R of I will be uniformly continuous.[11] As Beth pointed out, this means that the properties of the B under the analysis R of I will not be expressible in terms of classical propositional functions, for such a function could be used to construct a noncontinuous function (e.g., for such a propositional function F, let $f(b) = 0$ when $F(b)^* =$ False, and $f(b) = 1$ when $F(b)^* =$ True).

I have not been overly attentive to where phenomenology enters the matter. The relevant phenomenon (p,t,i) contains the "intuition" or, better, *insight,* that extensive geometric continua can be indefinitely subdivided, but that the quality of extensiveness is lost by taking a nested series of subdivisions, all nonempty, and passing to infinity. This is obvious. The contents of the phenomena do not sustain, and in fact speak against the idea that a point is "part" of an extensive continuum. (These contents can clearly be elaborated much further. I think the reader should be able to see that this is so. Such elaboration, however, would represent a distraction in this work.) This insight, clearly and strongly fulfilled by the phenomenon, limited our mathematical analysis of extensive continua, guiding us in the direction taken by Weyl. That is, our mathematical analysis represented our ("informal") reasoning about o_i, and it was regulated by $Val(p,t,i)$ in the form of the just-mentioned insight. Whether or not this mathematical analysis is *fully* motivated by this understanding Val, whether or not it is perfectly consistent or harmonious with it, only a more thorough phenomenological analysis can say. Such an analysis would begin by mak-

11. Arend Heyting, *Intuitionism* (Amsterdam, 1956), p. 46.

ing more explicit all of the details of the insight given above, at the same time seeking to clarify the phenomena underlying our understanding of the domain of points and point-sets. I think more thorough analyses would not alter the fact that *Val* (p,t,i) pushes us inexorably toward a nonclassical logic, although they would make clearer how this happens.

Example 2. o_i = the perfectly objectual, ego-independent physical world. Actually, the discussion is only nominally directed at "the physical world." What is important is that o_i be considered "perfectly objectual and ego-independent."

Let us suppose at hand a domain of truth-bearers adequately expressed in a language whose logical syntax is classical, i.e., connectives are truth-functional, quantifiers are objectual, and term-substitution is extensional. These truth-bearers are compelled by the interpretation of the logical syntax to be true or false, but not both, and to be so without any reference back to intensional conditions or to thinking, experiencing subjects. These truth-bearers are the "stable, independent" truth-bearers found necessary in Chapter I in order to have access to a stable, independent world—in order, at least, to frame such a world. This "presupposition" of classical logic has been widely noted.[12] Classical logic deserves to be explicated from this point of view, making this characterization rigorous, a characterization highly parasitic on the fact that classical logic generates a Lindenbaum algebra.[13] For a rigorous treatment of the following considerations, one would have to make such a characterization rigorous; it is surely intrinsically important to do so. Classical logic is extensionalizable and, e.g., intuitionistic logic is not, and therein are to be found the roots of the differences in the worlds that

12. E.g., Paul Bernays, "On Platonism in Mathematics," in *Philosophy of Mathematics,* ed. P. Benacerraf and H. Putnam, pp. 274–289.

13. J. L. Bell, and A. B. Slomsen, *Models and Ultraproducts* (Amsterdam, 1971), pp. 61f.

can be framed by truth-bearers expressible in the (interpreted) logical syntax of the one logic and not the other. For
the present I must satisfy myself by making the connection
between logic and phenomenological ontology, leaving the
rigorous explication of this connection for future work.

It was argued in Chapter I that stable, independent truth-
bearers are required in order to frame, and in order for us to
have perceptual and cognitive access to, a stable, independent
world. It was observed that, although there is no a priori reason why such truth-bearers cannot exist, and although we can
give cognitively contentual criteria for deciding their existence, we really cannot decide with certainty that we have
access to such a domain of truth-bearers.

It can be argued that it is a phenomenologically cogent fact
that what one means to be saying in uttering a declarative
sentence is typically a genuine, *observable* object (if usually
not intersubjectively observable). In fact, the person who
makes an assertion by using a sentence that is ambiguous or
vague typically will be able to decide which of the possible
"meanings" is correct. That is, *what is* (meant as being) *asserted* can stand somewhat apart from the sentence used to
make the assertion. This suggests that, at this very phenomenological level of consideration, there is an intensional entity,
what one means to be saying, that is more independent of the
language than any "eternal" sentence of the language, for it
seems that observation of the former can lead to an improved
choice of the latter. Such less dependent entities would better
stabilize truth.

Quine's "eternal sentences" cannot serve as fully independent, stable truth-bearers because of the always strong possibility of hidden ambiguity. Making the truth-bearers *what
one means to be saying* (we can sensibly do so because, as
I argued, the last is observable) gives us *more* stable truth-
bearers, but, as one might expect and as I will argue in IV.2,

one does not thereby obtain a perfectly stable domain of truth-bearers, because, e.g., there may be ambiguities one does not in fact know how to decide because of deficiencies in one's understanding of a world. Such considerations, however, do suggest something of interest—the more adequate and complete one's knowledge and understanding of a cognitively pursued stable, independent world, the more stable become the truth-bearers one has access to (e.g., the better one can see how to decide ambiguities, thereby discovering what one meant to say or—just as good and useful, because it is stabilizing—discovering what one ought to have said, thus assuring that, *ultimately,* the truth-bearers are stable). If we can be assured of stable, independent truth-bearers only in the long run, at the culmination of our cognitive efforts, what right do we have to use classical logic in the meantime? (Recall the discussion of classical logic given at the beginning of the example.) Inadequate truth-bearers are inadequately expressed by a language whose logical syntax is classical. Must this not lead to invalid inferences? Is there any justification for acting as if the available truth-bearers are nevertheless adequately expressed by sentences whose logical syntax is classical? Must we act in this way if we are to have access to a stable, independent world?

In his *Formal and Transcendental Logic,* Husserl carried out a critique of the correlative notions "absolutely existing object" and "absolute truths in themselves," [14] where 'absolute' connotes, in part, "independent of any ego." One conclusion he reached is that these notions have constitutive and regulative significance. One way of appreciating what this might mean is to consider that the notion might be capable of being used to frame "absolute," i.e., ego-independent, worlds, and thus in some measure hold the promise of mak-

14. Edmund Husserl, *Formal and Transcendental Logic,* trans. D. Cairns (The Hague, 1969), para. 73–81, 99.

ing such worlds accessible to us. Let us explore this point of view.

We need "absolute" or ego-independent truth-bearers in order to have access to an "absolute," independent world. But we do not seem to have immediate, certain access to such truth-bearers. We have two options:

(1) We can settle for relative, (ego-)dependent truth-bearers and thus relative, (ego-)dependent worlds. Ultimately, this means that our principles of logic would contain concessions to the ambiguity and vagueness of our truth-bearers.[15] Paul Bernays' inadequate criticism of intuitionistic logic [16] is, I think, trenchantly applied here: by assimilating into the principles of our logic the indeterminicies of our understanding, the deficiencies of the truth-bearers to which we do have access, we project those inadequacies and deficiencies onto the world being cognitively pursued, and there is something wrong about this if the world is not thus inadequate and deficient, if it is not, e.g., ego-dependent. Because our logical principles are designed to accommodate such deficiencies, they inspire no logical sense of outrage; in their accommodating way, they let flawed conceptions pass.

(2) Or, one can choose logical principles (classical logic) that demand independent truth-bearers. Once such principles have been adopted, there are two ways in which reasoning can be invalid: one makes a classically invalid inference or one reasons using inadequate truth-bearers, e.g., ambiguous or vague "eternal" sentences. That is, ambiguity or vagueness is *not* accommodated by the adopted, ruling logic. As with invalid inference, ambiguity or vagueness must be watched for. At least such ambiguity (and the instability and nonindependence it entails) is projected onto the domain

15. Max Black, *Margins of Precision* (Ithaca, N.Y., 1972), chap. 1.
16. Paul Bernays, "Bermerkungen zur Grundlagenfrage," in *Philosophie Mathematique,* ed. F. Gonseth (Paris, 1939), pp. 83–87.

being cognitively pursued only because it has been over-
looked and not because one's logical principles have accommodated it.

Clearly the negative considerations of (1) and the positive
considerations of (2) describe a reasonable course of action:
we frame an independent, stable world by choice of classical
logical syntax; this forces us constantly to strive toward secur-
ing independent, stable truth-bearers, leading us toward adequate cognition of an independent, stable world, a world to
which we would not have access if our logic had accommodated inadequate truth-bearers.

The choice of classical logic for physical theory can be
made on the foundation of considerations such as those just
given. The right to use such considerations is founded on the
way the relevant phenomena frame the physical world, on the
intention native to physical theory, to the thinking of physi-
cists, to the effect that physics aims at "the external world,"
a world fully objective and independent of our will and desire, a world that is ego-independent. For relevant (p,t,i),
$Val(p,t,i)$, on the ground of this intention, on this way of
framing or prehending o_i, *requires that physical reasoning
not make any moves construing the physical world as ego-
dependent*. (The reader is referred to I.2 for Frege's "intentional analysis" of the ego-independence of "the eternal
world.") It is in this respect that $Val(p,t,i)$ leads to the justification given above for using classical logic.

The main difficulty we face is that the above-mentioned
intention is neither the sole constituent of the relevant i of
(p,t,i) nor the sole power governing what might rightly be admitted as part of the understanding $Val(p,t,i)$. A much deeper
probing of the relevant (p,t,i), at least along the lines begun
by Husserl in his *Crisis of the European Sciences and Transcendental Phenomenology*, is required in order to secure a
fuller understanding $Val(p,t,i)$ making more explicit and

precise the sense in which o_i is objective and independent, and at the same time showing that p has a right to assert the existence of o_i, the physical world (see III.2).

In any case, the rather minimal phenomenological or intentional analysis given above justifying classical logic, the analysis that says we want our physical theory to frame a perfectly objective, external, independent world, serves to provide reasons better than arbitrary for denying the claim that physics is aimed at a purely empiricist or verificationist world. As Carl Hempel has in effect shown, the requirement that natural-scientific truth, and thus physical truth, coincide with empirical verification is in conflict with classical logic.[17] Classical quantification theory allows the formation of sentences that cannot be assigned empirical criteria deciding them. Similar considerations have led Myhill, Grzegorczyk, and Prawitz to suggest that intuitionistic logic is the correct logic for physics.[18] Their analyses however, must ignore that element in (p,t,i) framing the physical world o_i as something external and ego-independent. To employ intuitionistic logic (under, e.g., the provability interpretation) is to project onto the physical world the trait of being dependent on what p can empirically verify.

A reduction of physical theory to a theory about sense-perceived objects could and, given the native intention of the physicist, must be regarded *as merely formal,* as not carrying along enough of what is meant or intended. The observation theory would not have the character of being a theory of the

17. Carl Hempel, "Empiricist Criteria of Cognitive Significance," in his *Aspects of Scientific Explanation* (New York, 1965), pp. 102–107.

18. John Myhill, "Empirical Meaningfulness and Intuitionistic Logic," *Philosophy and Phenomenological Research,* 33 (1972), 186–191; A. Grzegorczyk, "A Philosophically Plausible Formal Interpretation of Intuitionistic Logic," *Indagationes Mathematicae,* 26 (1964), 596–601; Dag Prawitz, "Constructive Semantics," in *Proceedings of the First Scandinavian Logic Symposium* (Uppsala, 1970), pp. 96–114.

same domain that the original theory had the character of being a theory of, for the original theory seemed to be about entities only obliquely or even accidentally related to experience. To give an analogous example, consider the proof-theoretic inter-interpretability of classical and intuitionistic number theory. Each can be finitistically proved to be a "subsystem" of the other.[19] If one chose, one could without loss do classical number theory inside intuitionistic number theory (or rather, inside its formalized version). But no one would say that "the numbers" of classical number theory are identical with "the numbers" of intuitionistic number theory. Intuitionistic numbers, after all, are intuitive constructions obtained by a certain abstractive reflection on the subjective movement of time. Whatever numbers are from the classical or Platonist point of view (e.g., classes of classes, categories of certain chains), they are certainly not such things from the intuitionistic point of view. One cannot argue that the apparent differences in intention between classical and intuitionistic number theory are shown by the inter-interpretability results to be illusory, for to say this ignores the very different *Val*'s at work. It is difficult to reply to someone who is convinced that something that does not make a formal difference makes no real difference, and so the differences in the *Val*'s are illusory when the resulting formal theories are in some strong sense inter-interpretable. But one can make the following reply: The formalist does not take into account the sources of the formal systems. From this point of view one might observe that classical and intuitionistic mathematics had not been pushed far enough to make essentially formal differences appear (viz., perhaps the respective *Val*'s had not been cultivated deeply enough to justify theories in which the essential differences appear as incomparable formal dif-

19. S. C. Kleene, *Introduction to Metamathematics* (New York, 1962), para. 81.

ferences). We get mutually inconsistent formal systems when we inflate the respective number theories into respective full theories of "the real number continuum" ("full," i.e., not merely analysis qua second-order number theory). Perhaps, in the case of the physical theory translatable into a (sensory) observation theory, if one had worked out the original intention and had more fully explored and exploited the relevant *Val,* one would have formed a compelling physical theory strikingly irreducible to such an observation theory.

Having physical theory framed in classical logic may lead to truths founded outside of perception. Such truths would then be justified on the grounds motivating the choice of classical logic, viz., that (p,t,i) $(o_i =$ the physical world) frames an objective, ego-independent world.

All these matters can and must be clarified on the ground of an increasingly deeper analysis and understanding $Val(p,t,i)$. I think enough has been said, however, to make clear that the phenomena give us compelling, nonempirical reasons for adopting classical logic.

I will try to say briefly where phenomenology enters in Example 2, above. The consideration that the predicates we use in the informal formulation of our scientific theories approach the degree of precision required by classical logic as our knowledge evolves (classical logic thus generating a regulative ideal determining the final form of theories) is the property of many philosophers, few of them phenomenologists. The question remains: why adopt this ideal? Phenomenological reflection answers the question in part. Such reflection reveals (see, e.g., the intentional analysis given by Frege discussed in I.2) that our prehension of the physical world involves an important element construing the physical world as an objective, external, ego-independent reality. This revelation, however, is so easily won that it hardly gives much interest to phenomenology. The genuine contribution here of phenomenological reflection is that already made in Chapter III and applied in Chapter IV. The contribution essentially consists of the antireductionist, antimetaphysical considerations underlying phenomenological ontology: we are justified in asserting that a world W exists as it "appears" (as it is projected in one's conception (p,t,i)) provided that the relevant $Val(p,t,i)$ is constrained and rich enough to sustain increasingly complete cognitive apprehension of W. Thus, to refer back to the example from Gödel in the Introduction, we are justified in using classical logic in reasoning about the domain of set theory, thus construing it as a well-determined reality, which in itself decides all questions about it, as long as the relevant $Val(p,t,i)$'s show the way to a more complete, nonarbitrary, "rational" cognitive apprehension of the domain of sets.

It is important to observe that our attitude toward the existence of W is not an *"als ob,"* "as if" attitude. Rather, if W satisfies the criterion for asserting the existence of a world, then we will find the thought of its existence compelling, for W will stand before the mind as an objective presence. To the extent that an element of "as if" intrudes, to that extent will W seem chimerical.

Quine argues in *Philosophy of Logic* that logical truth is founded on two things: grammar and truth.[20] "A sentence is logically true if all sentences with that logical structure are true." Quine specifically *rejects* the idea "that it is language that makes logical truths true—purely language, and nothing to do with the nature of the world." He continues by explaining the close connection between language and logic. First, different admissible adjustments in the "grammaticiza-

20. W. V. Quine, *Philosophy of Logic*, pp. 58–60, 95–100. These passages are the source of the quotations in the following three paragraphs.

tion" of a language vary the distinction between logical truth and other truth. There is something arbitrary about whether a sentence is true by nature of language or true by the nature of the world, and this suggests that 'true' has an odd meaning. Second, logic is tied to translation. If someone p claims false what for me has the form of a logically true sentence s, then I am obligated to suppose either that p is an idiot or that p is not taking s in the same way I am. But this does not make the truth of s dependent completely on language, for any obvious truths (such as "It is raining" when it is) would have the same effect. Third, when we talk about logic we seem to be talking about language. But,

the truth predicate is already present and doing an active job of separating logic from language. The truth predicate serves the crucial purpose . . . of disquotation. Logical theory, despite its heavy dependence on talk of language, is already world-oriented rather than language-oriented; and the truth predicate makes it so.

The effect of such considerations is to push forward the suggestion that it is the world that is decisive for truth. Espousing his doctrine of gradualism and the maxim of minimum mutilation, given his convictions about the primacy of empirical evidence, Quine holds that logical principles are obliquely regulated by, and are ultimately confirmed by sense-experience, and so also that "logic is in principle no less open to revision than quantum mechanics or the theory of relativity."

The two examples we have considered show the following: (1) Logic is an equivocal subject. Thus, we can not accept Quine's claim of "the universal applicability of logic, its impartial participation in all the sciences." (2) There are two reasons why we can not agree that "logical truths will qualify as obvious, in the behavioral sense in which I am using the term, or potentially obvious." (a) Logical truths are not obvious in general, for we have no hope of a decision procedure, so that the behavioral sense of 'obvious' here is obscure to me. *More importantly,* (b) we realize that different objective domains may require different logics, so that when we find someone denying, say, the law of the excluded middle, we may not unhesitatingly construe him as mad or ourselves as mistranslating his speech. (It is, of course, a *very* different matter when we confront someone denying the law of noncontradiction!) In this case, we must try to consider toward what objective domain his talk is directed. (3) I think it is important that, with Quine, we give no special status to "logical truth" as opposed to "truth," or, rather, we do not allow "truth by fiat" or "truth by language alone." However much language prepares the way, it is the considered world that is decisive for what is true versus what is untrue. As I have explained, one must justify the choice of logical laws or logical syntax by reference to a considered world. I agree with Quine on this point. But I (4) disagree with him on how the choice is to be made. Our examples show how it is possible to rightly and compellingly make a choice among logics on the foundation of *nonempirical,* phenomenological observations. Phenomenology thus points the way to a nonempirical, transcendental foundation for logic.

IV.2. Informal Reasoning and Truth-Bearers

This section investigates a gap between informal reasoning and logically formal reasoning. The gap is filled by a phenomenologically appreciated phase in our reasoning which is in a sense "logic-free."

In Richard Cartwright's usage, a sentence is 'incomplete'

when "the meaning of the sentence is such as to permit utterances of the sentence to vary as to the statement made." [21] 'It is raining' is incomplete. Quine's eternal sentences, e.g., '7 is prime', are presumably complete. In order to support propositionalist doctrines, one might hope to show that utterance situations determine complete sentences, so that *what* is asserted can be identified in terms of (1) a complete sentence and (2) the specification of the language in which the complete sentence is formed. J. F. Thomson, in his consideration of these matters, argued that there are serious problems with giving complete identity criteria for languages and that there are problems about ambiguity.[22] Consider an occasion of asserting something. That situation may

(1)   determine a complete sentence *s*, but

(2)   *s* has an ambiguity which either

(2.1) is not recognizable at the time, or

(2.2) is such that there is nothing in the situation of utterance to decide possible resolution of the ambiguity.

Thomson gives the example of the child who says 'Cats climb trees':

Imagine a small child to watch while a cat is treed by a dog and to announce 'Cats climb trees'. A logician or a linguist might wonder what he himself would or might mean, intend to assert, if he uttered that sentence. That some cats do or have? That all do? That all can? Or perhaps that most can? But no one will want to hold that an intention of that degree of specificity must have existed in the child's mind.[23]

The child may simply not know which of these he was asserting, and yet something significant was being said, e.g., a playmate may have "perfectly" understood him.

21. Richard Cartwright, "Propositions," in *Analytic Philosophy, First Series*, ed. R. Butler (Oxford, 1956), pp. 85f.

22. J. F. Thomson, "Truth-Bearers and the Trouble about Propositions," *Journal of Philosophy*, 66 (1969), 737–747.

23. Ibid., p. 744.

The same sort of situation occurs repeatedly in ordinary and intellectual life. For example, a theoretical chemist who talks about "the energy of electron-pair bonds," "resonance energies," or "atomic orbitals" is typically saying things that are rather ambiguous when one tries to think them through in terms of theoretical physics. The chemist understands himself "perfectly"; the problem comes only when he is faced with fine physical distinctions which, given his intellectual development and the intellectual development of his science, he is not quite prepared to deal with from the point of view of chemistry. After all, if one cannot be understood (necessarily, not even by one's own self) when one's theories are not perfectly delineated, then there can be no possibility of achieving full, good theory, for all theory formation begins in the midst of sometimes great confusion, in which there is nevertheless an order (otherwise that confusion can never be found interesting and will not inspire future, less confused theory). The chemist's theories of things such as "resonance energies" can be changed or completed in different inequivalent ways (relative to physical theory), but when he talks of such things as "resonance energies" he may still be speaking intelligibly without knowing which of those theoretical alternatives is the right or best one to adopt. Even if he chose one of the alternatives and built much of his life's work on it, it would still be possible for him sensibly (albeit, regretfully) to go back and start afresh if he found that indeed the path he had taken was the wrong path.

If A asserts that p, and if 'p' has substituted for it an ambiguous sentence in the sense of either (2.1) or (2.2), ambiguities which cannot be resolved on the basis of the occasion of utterance, then the entity which is asserted must in some sense be blurred or fuzzy. A propositionalist, says Thomson, would say that on any occasion of asserting something, including the occasion where p could be read as either some purportedly unambiguous, complete P_1 or as some other purportedly unambiguous, complete p_2 and there is nothing in the situation of assertive utterance to decide between p_1 and p_2, either p_1 or p_2 is nevertheless actually asserted. Thomson can find no basis for making this claim. Indeed, by dint of the discussion of ambiguity, there seems to be strong support for claiming that what is asserted is a blurred entity.

One can say something a little stronger: What is asserted, if not always a blurred entity, is at least such that there are no general principles (i.e., principles with parameters for arbitrary assertions) for deciding whether or not an apparently complete sentence is actually complete and unambiguous. Nor can we expect, given arbitrary assertions plus their situations of utterance, rules determining unique, complete sentences. Thus, the content of an assertion is not a formal or strictly objective affair. An assertion may appear ambiguous against the background of a grid of more refined concepts than were available at the time of utterance, and yet I may have "perfectly" understood myself and may have been "perfectly" understood at the time of utterance. What I have asserted may appear blurred because it is irresolvable by any convincing general principles or objective criteria for sorting out ambiguities (as the child who said 'Cats climb trees' will appear to be uttering nonsense to someone who demands that the logical structure of all utterances be explicit, or as the chemist will appear hopelessly sloppy and careless and rather unintelligible to the theoretical physicist). It may also be intelligible, however, and may produce understanding in a situation where one's insights and intuitions have not yet matured, or at least where they have not matured to the point where more refined and less ambiguous assertions are possible, where indeed those precious insights and intuitions might be totally lost and all progress in thought ruined if too much precision were demanded.

Thomson's remarks and the examples and discussion above reveal the existence of states of mind that are deficient in clarity relative to some ideal language of complete sentences (perhaps some logically perfect language, where all concepts are refined to their utmost), and yet such states of mind may be sound and full of understanding, understanding by which such perfection of thought may someday be achieved. There was algebra before Vieta and Descartes, and there were sound deductions before Frege. To be prelogical is not to be alogical.

I will now phenomenologically examine these states of mind, which indeed underlie *all* good thinking, by means of a sketch of a phenomenological analysis of an ordinary situation involving such states of mind.

I am watching a rapidly moving train. I attempt to describe as much of the train as I can. Now I focus on the content of my awareness as I am describing the moving train and I immediately discern two contents of that awareness:

(1) my interest is focused on the passing train, and

(2) I find myself putting into words what I see.

Call (1) 'the attentive focus' and (2) 'the putting into words'.

Consider 'the attentive focus.' I am focused on the moving train. To be so focused on such an object which at any moment extends in part beyond my field of vision and yet remains taken as the same, despite rapid alteration of the contents of my visual field, I must possess a sense of unity, some overarching awareness of a unity holding my attention upon and tracing and renewing the sense of the boundaries of the train, putting together the continuous phases of presentation as presentations of the same thing. Clearly it must be this sense of unity that determines what in my visual field has to do with the train and what does not and so regulates what I will and will not admit as descriptions of the train as I am now perceiving it.

Consider 'the putting into words.' As I attend to the train, perceived aspects of its features begin, so-to-speak, to flow into words. Descriptive phrases and sentences form, usually spontaneously. Their forming is clearly guided by an underlying sense of awareness of appropriateness, acting, when needed, as censor—irrelevant phrases, wrong or poorly nuanced words, or emerging sentences with disastrous syntax are typically canceled. There may be hesitations in which I seek out the correct word or turn of phrase. Thus we notice two further aspects of the awareness of describing:

(3) a three-fold sense of correctness, and

(4) a meaning-to-say intention.

Accompanying any occurrence of a putting into words in the context of describing the object (the train), one can discern three modes of awareness of correctness:

(SC1) there is a sense of correctness of the emerging sentence as a description of the object of attentive focus (the object one means to be describing),

(SC2) there is an awareness that one is saying what one means to be saying, and

(SC3) there is an awareness that the emergent sentence makes sense, e.g., that it is sufficiently grammatical.

(SC2) draws our attention to two further features:

(5) what one means to be saying, and

(6) what the words or sentences one produces say or suggest in relation to what one means to be saying.

I will consider only (5) here. (6) is included for completeness.

What one means to be saying can be regarded as an object, for it certainly constrains thought (there are some things which one clearly does not mean to be saying) and it has its own mode of "being perceived." I am not talking about something altogether strange and unfamiliar—and certainly not about a merely hypothetical entity. Such objects, what one means to be saying, are clearly in view in those situations where one finds oneself saying "what I meant to say was . . ." or "I know what I want (mean) to say, but words fail me. . . . " What one means to say in some sense hovers before one, just out of grasp. Such a "grasp" is achieved by finding a sentence such that in uttering it one clearly seems to be saying what one means to be saying. (As in the case of sense-perception, there is room here for illusion.) Although the entity, the meaning-to-say, hovers just out of grasp, it may be brought to fuller perception by hitting upon the right turns of phrase. Certainly it may often be conveyed or communicated without succeeding in saying exactly what one means.

The meaning-to-say qua object behaves very much like an idea for solving some scientific problem or for opening up an area of investigation, an idea which jumps into one's mind improperly dressed in words, but which attracts words to itself in abundance, words that one knows to be not quite right to capture the idea, as when one is aware that one has not said what one means to be saying. One may also succeed in conveying an idea to others even though it is badly articulated. In fact, one may convey the idea very well and perhaps even better in a vague language rather than in some ideally precise language.

If what is at stake is the logical nature of assertions, the resolution of logical ambiguities (e.g., the decision whether the use of 'not' or 'for some' should be classical or intuitionistic, or whatever), then perhaps there is a core of understanding and a corresponding core of assertion which is logically underdetermined (e.g., the 'not' or 'for some' is still seminal, capable of conceiving a host of different interpretations), a core of assertion powerful enough to suggest the logical meaning we will in future decide upon, but also now productive of rich communications of our ideas. Perhaps if we would stop imposing our current logical dispositions on ordinary language, we could clearly see that ordinary language is such a logically plastic language, the vehicle for logically underdetermined assertions which can nevertheless be shaped to convey, if not precisely express, precise meanings when the time for logical perfection of our thoughts comes. Perhaps ordinary language is logically neutral, but also plastic enough for us to formulate differing logics or concepts of truth. The readiness with which ordinary language absorbs our current logical dispositions and gives the illusion of rigidly embodying them suggests that this is so. Thus the logical plasticity of ordinary language and that power of our thinking to come to grips with and soundly think through sound ideas which are still intuitive or badly expressed, a power without which science would be impossible, are the sources of our freedom to adopt the logic we ought to adopt. The phenomenological problem is to reach a full understanding of the character and potentialities of the logically underdetermined sphere of reasoning, which shapes and motivates the logically determinate sphere from which scientific theory emerges.

IV.3. The Problem of the Diversity of Concepts of Truth

Logical truths can not be false. Thus, if there are to be different ("complete") logics, there must be different concepts of truth [24] which the different logics might be construed as embodying, and thus different categories of worlds for which

24. Trivially, without the completeness condition, one could divide a concept of truth among subsystems of a logic.

the truths *are true*. The idea that sound and intelligible logics should embody concepts of truth emerged recently in Quine, albeit not with full approbation.[25] Charles Parsons, hoping to shed light on substitutional quantification theory, attempted to cultivate the idea that a sound and intelligible logic must embody a concept of truth (or, equivalently, a concept of existence).[26] From another point of view, the importance of considering logics only under interpretations, which is at root the same issue, was brought out by Richard Grandy.[27] The failure to appreciate the connection between logics and concepts of truth has led to some seriously mistaken work in logic. For example, in a review of K. Bowen's "An Extension of the Intuitionistic Propositional Calculus," C. A. Smorynski took Bowen to task on just this point.[28] Bowen proposed a new "intuitionistic" logical connective by means of a formal construction with Gentzen-style deduction schemes and proved that the proposed connective would not be defined in terms of the other connectives. Smorynski argued clearly and forcefully that Bowen did not show that this connective was intuitionistic, i.e., that it had an interpretation in terms of the intuitionistic concept of truth. Failing such an interpretation, there can be no assurance that reasoning cast in an intuitionistic language extended by Bowen's "connective" will be valid, that it will preserve truth, even if the resulting system is formally consistent.

What we need in the foundations of logic is a clear and convincing analysis of the notion "concepts of truth" ade-

25. W. V. Quine, "Existence and Quantification," in *Ontological Relativity and Other Essays* (New York, 1969), p. 113.

26. Charles Parsons, "A Plea for Substitutional Quantification Theory."

27. Richard Grandy, "Some Remarks about Logical Form," *Nous*, 8 (1974), 157–164.

28. C. Smorynski, review of Bowen's "An Extension of the Intuitionistic Propositional Calculus," in *Mathematical Reviews*, 45 (1973), no. 3161.

quate to justify individual logics and clearly to distinguish among them according to the concept of truth they embody. Given such an analysis, we will no longer blindly have to regiment our discourse within the pattern of one logic or another; having a battery of concepts of truth at hand and presumably a full knowledge of their effects, we will be able to choose one pattern of regimentation over another with full knowledge of what we are doing and of the consequences of our act.

How does a logical syntax become interpreted? How does a concept of truth enter into that syntax? In his article "The Concept of Truth in Formalized Languages," Tarski presents a forceful answer to these questions. There are two problems. The first is to decide when any concept of truth defined for a (formal) language L is adequate, when we have in a way coherent with the notion "truth" adequately said when, and only when, the sentences of L are true. The second is to learn how to define a concept of truth for (formal) language L which meets the test of adequacy. (Of course, it is not to be expected that every formal language can be thus interpreted.)

There are certain difficulties with Tarski's solution to the first problem. In the previously mentioned article, he argued that any adequate explanation of truth for a language L must satisfy what he calls 'Convention T'.[29] (Briefly, Convention T says that an explanation of "truth-in-L" is adequate only if one can derive in the metatheory embodying the explanation of "truth-in-L" all sentences of the form

(T) n is true iff s,

where for s one substitutes a sentence of the metalanguage and for n one substitutes a canonical name for a sentence of L, where the sentence substituted for s is an "interpretation" for the sentence named by the name substituted for n.)

29. A. Tarski, "The Concept of Truth in Formalized Languages," in *Logic, Semantics, and Metamathematics* (Oxford, 1956), p. 187.

This is unsatisfactory because, as Tarski shows, the law of excluded middle is imposed on the object language L.[30] Trivially, if, as Tarski does, the 'iff' in (T) is interpreted classically, letting 'Tn' express "n is true," 'Fn', "n is false," and '$-$', truth functional negation, then

(1) Tn iff s (Premise $-(T)$)

(2) $-Tn$ iff $-s$ (from 1)   (3) Fn iff $-s$ (meaning of "$-$")

---

(4) $-Tn$ iff Fn (from 2,3)

(5) $-Tn \rightarrow Fn$ (from 4)

(6) Tn v Fn (from 5) QED

But the law of the excluded middle does not in general hold, for example, in the case of language interpreted by a constructive concept of truth, an intuitionistic syntax. Wang has observed other difficulties with Convention T.[31]

Although Tarski's adequacy condition Convention T is thus in doubt and clearly wrong for many nonclassical logical languages, his definition of truth for the languages he considers (and which definition he hoped to prove adequate under Convention T) is clearly highly flexible and, most importantly, intuitively sound. The idea is to define truth in a language L thus: [32]

n is true-in-L iff n is satisfied.

(The phrase 'n is satisfied' is to be defined recursively in the intuitive meanings of the logical operations.[33]) The 'n is satisfied' is intended to mean, "satisfied by the objects in such and such a world." Thus, another sort of adequacy condition is called for which is not discussed by Tarski—that the explanation of "n is satisfied" be adjusted to the nature of the considered world, that sentences which are "satisfied" under this explanation do say something true about that world. It is

30. Ibid., p. 197.

31. H. Wang, "Certain Predicates Defined by Induction Schemata," *Journal of Symbolic Logic*, 18 (1953), 49–59.

32. Tarski, p. 195.   33. Ibid., p. 193.

possible for an explanation of satisfaction consistent with classical logical syntax to guarantee the "satisfaction" of sentences not true in a constructive or intuitionistic world. As long as it can be maintained that there is only one logic, this second adequacy condition poses no problem, for that logic will a fortiori be adequate for any scientific theory of an objective domain. But since we showed in this work that there are grounds for asserting the existence of objective domains requiring different logics, we must impose this second, profoundly difficult, adequacy condition, viz., that the concept of truth must be "appropriate" for the objective domain (world) under consideration. IV.1 presented examples showing that we can, sometimes as a consequence of (phenomenological) analysis, detect when a concept of truth is "appropriate" for an objective domain.

The idea of an interpreted logical syntax emerged in the preceding pages. An interpreted logical syntax is a formal logical language (a list of symbols together with rules saying which symbol strings are well-formed formulas). Assuming that the class of well-formed formulas is recursively defined, the well-formed formulas are assigned truth conditions recursively in the logical symbols. In this sense, an interpreted logical syntax can be thought of as "embodying" a concept of truth.

But what counts as a recursive assignment of truth conditions leading to a logical syntax embodying a "genuine" concept of truth, a concept of truth determining truth conditions whose satisfaction yields truth about some world? Tarski's Convention T was intended in part to solve this problem. We have seen that, because of the diversity of concepts of truth and interpreted logics, it does not. Convention T does not take care of the concept of truth in intuitionistic logic. (It

also fails, in a sense, for substitutional quantification theory.[34])
Also, since Convention T forces us to explain a concept of
truth in terms of our talk of a world, it does not provide us
with an understanding of the relation among worlds, truth,
and language which covers worlds requiring nonclassical
logics.

This is a difficult problem, and I must leave it open. But
I will conclude with some remarks about what would not
count as a solution and how phenomenological work suggests
a way to an answer.

A retreat to a purely formal point of view must be inadequate. A merely formal logic, where logical operations are
"explained" in terms of inference rules, is inadequate, for
reasons pointed out (albeit ironically) in A. N. Prior's "The
Runabout Inference Ticket"; according to the analysis of
N. D. Belnap's commentary on Prior in "Tonk, Plonk, and
Plink," [35] one needs at least a demonstration of "consistency"
and "uniqueness." Even that is not enough, however, unless
one can abide purely positivist criteria for choosing among
logics (e.g., considerations of fruitfulness and simplicity).
Rather we have to make clear that, whatever inferences we
allow in our logics, they take us from truths about considered
worlds to truths about those worlds. A canonical semantics
that cuts across a host of logics such as the semantics given in
Chang and Keisler's *Continuous Model Theory*, probably
won't do, for while it provides an interpretation for, say, intuitionistic logic, it does not present us with the semantics in
terms of the intuitionistic concept of truth.

Tarski's articles III, V, and XII in his *Logic, Semantics,*

34. John Wallace, "Convention T and Substitutional Quantification,"
Nous, 5 (1971), 199–211.
35. Both articles are in P. F. Strawson, ed., *Philosophical Logic* (Oxford, 1956).

and Metamathematics are of interest in narrowing the scope of our researches. We ultimately want logics capable of formulating deductive theories. Although these articles are predominately formalistic in flavor, and slanted toward classical logic, if one ignores the axioms unique to classical logic, then perhaps it can be argued that in them Tarski gives minimal formal conditions for what a logical syntax must be to serve as a foundation for formulating deductive theories. (There does not seem to exist a formal syntax for some of the logics discussed in Chang and Keisler's *Continuous Model Theory*.) This would be extremely helpful in limiting the classes of logics we would have to consider as possible candidates for interpretation. For such logics there is an obvious sense of 'consistency', as Tarski shows.

. To solve the larger problem of the range of "interpreted logical syntaxes" we thus require purely logical investigations into the shape of deductive logics and possible ways of defining logics in a purely formal manner. The Prawitz/ Gentzen systems of natural deduction perhaps provide the best means to achieve this end. But such investigations must be supplemented by studies relating formal logics to worlds, thus interpreting the former. For this it seems we require a theory of all possible worlds. Such a theory, however, typically begins with a logic (possible worlds are defined, e.g., in terms of complete, consistent sets of wffs in the considered logic). What we require is a theory of possible worlds that does not define the worlds in terms of logics. Since analyses of adequate understandings $Val(p,t,i)$ provide criteria for deciding the existence of worlds and, as we saw in IV.1, the promise of also deciding among logics, perhaps what we need is a theory of all possible worlds obtained from a theory of all possible adequate $Val(p,t,i)$, which Husserl calls 'a transcendental theory of the constitutive Apriori', a main theme of his *Formal and Transcendental Logic*. It is hard to say what such a theory would look like and thus hard to say how far we are from it. But I think it reasonable to suggest that logic stands to gain much from the effort toward developing such a theory. One would certainly end with an answer to a variation on Føllesdal's question "Quine or Husserl?" Viz., "Is Logic empirical or nonempirical (transcendental)?" I think that the considerations of IV.1 suggest that we can *not* say "Empirical!" with equanimity, even if phenomenology does not constitute the least eristic path to an answer; but this, too, remains to be seen.

Some precise, mathematical work promises to shed light on these matters. Consider the following problems, Problem n being reduced, at least in part, to Problem $n + 1$:

Problem 1. Given a concept of truth, to determine the limits of its validity;

Problem 2. Perhaps by extending Tarski's ideas, to argue that concepts of truth can be explicated in terms of interpreted logical syntaxes;

Problem 3. To explain the origin of the logical operations appearing in interpreted logical syntaxes;

Problem 4. In order to secure adequate insight to solve the last, we must solve the so-called "adequacy problem" for known logics, viz.,

Given a logic L, and a set S of logical operations of L, we say that S is *adequate for* L if every logical operation of L is explicitly definable in terms of S. The *adequacy problem* for a logic L is the problem of showing that a certain set S of logical operations is adequate for L.[36]

36. Jeffrey Zucker, "The Adequacy Problem for Inferential Logic," University of Utrecht Mathematics Preprints, Preprint Number 37, November 1976. I had solved the problem for minimal logic. In this and a forthcoming preprint Zucker solves the adequacy problem of "intuitionistic" logic and classical logic.

Appendix: Husserl's Theory of Noematic Nuclei

I construe phenomena as conceptions (p,t,i). Husserl construes phenomena as noemata (determinate *Sinne* by virtue of which acts of consciousness refer to objects of acts). Conceptions (p,t,i) are composed of acts. In my view, a principal application of phenomenology is to find by reflection "rational" theoretical unities in conceptions. We *can* do this; much can be learned simply by observing *how* we can. It is on this basis that the naive phenomenology presented here has interest. In my opinion, Husserl is attempting to give ("transcendental") foundations to naive phenomenology. In his view, rational unities, acts of higher order, scientific theories, can emerge because the lower order acts of consciousness involve "meanings" (noemata) that make rational syntheses possible. Thus Husserl is able to explain "transcendentally" phenomenological facts we have discovered *naively*. How good his explanations are depends on how well one can accommodate intensional entities (noemata, noematic *Sinne*). I will briefly show that Husserl does find the roots of our $Val(p,t,i)$, provided one accepts his reconstruction of phenomena in terms of noemata.

The careful student of Husserl's texts will find my identification of the $Val(p,t,i)$'s Procrustean, not fully grounded; but perhaps it will also suggest that what Husserl was doing

and what I am doing are not entirely different. My own feeling about my "identification" is that it suggests that there is
much to be learned from Husserl and that there is still much
room for the development of a refined understanding of the
entities I discuss, an understanding that could be achieved
by deepening my analyses vis-à-vis Husserl's analyses of related phenomenological entities.

Husserl studies what are in effect $Val(p,t,i)$'s in *Ideas*. He
calls them 'noematic nuclei'.

Within the *complete* noema . . . we must separate out as essentially different strata which group themselves about a *central
nucleus*, the sheer "objective *Sinn*", that which in our examples
was something that could everywhere be described in purely
identical objective terms [objective = without reference to
Δ-predicates] because in specifically different though parallel
experiences [e.g., different perceptions of the same thing] there
could be an identical element.[1]

And also:

Even in the case of higher level noeses [e.g., the justification of
theories] . . . there figures on the noematic side a central nucleus
which at first obtrudes itself prominently, the "meant objectivity
as such [as meant]." . . . There also this central noema must be
understood in precisely that modified objective state in which it
is in fact a noema, the consciously known as such.[2]

In the contents of a noema (phenomenon) we find many
things ascribed to or predicated of o_i: "The predicates are
predicates of 'something', and this 'something' belongs together with the predicates, and clearly inseparably, to the
nucleus in question: it is the central point of unification." [3]
'Something' is in quotes to indicate that Husserl is *not* talking about the actual object o_i of an act, but about the fact

1. Edmund Husserl, *Ideas*, trans. W. R. B. Gibson (New York, 1969),
p. 266.
2. Ibid., p. 271.   3. Ibid., p. 365.

that the ascriptions have the *character* of being ascribed to something, viz., to o_i. That is, the noematic nucleus gives to the ascriptions the *character* of being rightly ascribed to one, and only one, thing (although deeper analysis might prove the ascribed character undeserved).

The nucleus "is the nodal point of connection for predicates, their "bearer", but in no wise their unity in the sense in which any system of connection might be called a unity." [4] Husserl is saying that the nucleus is a unity of predicates or ascriptions, but it is not true that the nucleus unifies them because it is *a set* of the ascriptions. Rather, the nucleus must have a unity specifying an object o_i to which the predicates are rightly or justifiably ascribed. It is the noematic nucleus that enables p to see (insightfully) that he is justified in making such and such ascriptions and whose apprehension provides such justification. "There detaches . . . as the central noematic phase: the 'object', the 'objective unity' (*Objekt*), the 'selfsame', the 'determinable subject of possible predicates'—the pure X in abstraction from all predicates—and it disconnects itself *from* these predicates, or more accurately from the predicate-noemata." [5] This nuclear part of the collective noema is a conceptual structure determining an "objective unity," "self-sameness," "the pure X in abstraction from all predicates"—it must provide a principle of objecthood, a principle of individuation, having significance "in abstraction from ascribed predicates" (i.e., independent of any particular scientific theory of the object).

If an act can be seen to be genuinely concerned with and directed toward an object, then such a principle of objecthood $Val(p,t,i)$ (noematic nucleus or nuclear objective unity) must be found to be part of the content of the considered noema (phenomenon). To the extent that we can not find any compelling "nuclear unity" we must have serious misgivings

4. Ibid., p. 365.   5. Ibid., p. 365–366.

about whether what we are cognitively pursuing can continue to inspire and sustain scientific investigation and theory, i.e., whether we are pursuing anything objective or "real" at all. If the relevant phenomena did not possess such a noematic nucleus $Val(p,t,i)$ then one must regard the pretense of i to be referring to something independent of p's will and desire as an unjustified pretense, as a pretense which could have no significance for p. The reason is that, lacking criteria $Val(p,t,i)$, p would fail to be compelled to regard any assertions (viz., those that would be in conformity with Val) as being justifiably asserted as true of o_i; the latter would have only the most ephemeral or mystical reality for p:

As every intentional experience has a noema and therein a *Sinn* through which it is related to the object, so, inversely, everything that we call by the name *Object*, that of which we speak, what we see before us as reality, hold to be possible or probable, think of in however vague a way, is in so far already an object of consciousness; and this means that whatever the world or reality may be or be called must be represented within the limits of real and possible consciousness of corresponding *Sinne* and positions [ascriptions], filled more or less with intuitional [e.g., sensual, prooflike] content.[6]

If p is to be justified in calling an object 'real', then this is because the relevant phenomena provide concepts, noematic nuclei $Val(p,t,i)$, giving conditions (on Δ-sentences) determining when the truth of a Δ-sentence $Δ(p,s(i),b)$ is grounds for p asserting the truth of $s(i)$ and where the full apprehension of Val would provide (at least in the long run) full justification for using such grounds.

In realizing that phenomena related to objects of scientific investigation must contain fully compelling nuclei $Val(p,t,i)$ determining the conditions identifying their objects (principles $Val(p,t,i)$ of observation and of justifiable considerations

6. Ibid., p. 374.

regulating and constraining what one might rationally assert of o_i), and in realizing that a phenomenon without such a core cannot be in possession of an object, or at least cannot provide the foundation for scientific cognition of its object, in realizing that indeed the object of the phenomenon must then have the character of being "unreal," of being without "scientific reality," we are brought to phenomenological ontology (in the sense used in Chapter III).

Bibliography

Bell, J. L., and A. B. Slomsen. *Models and Ultraproducts*. Amsterdam: North Holland Publishing Company, 1971.

Benacerraf, Paul. "Mathematical Truth." *Journal of Philosophy*, 70 (1973), 661–679.

———, and H. Putnam, eds. *Philosophy of Mathematics: Selected Readings*. Englewood Cliffs, N.J.: Prentice-Hall, 1964.

Bernays, Paul. "Bermerkungen zur Grundlagenfrage." In *Philosophie Mathematique*, ed. F. Gonseth. Paris: Hermann, 1939, pp. 83–87.

———. "On Platonism in Mathematics." In *Philosophy of Mathematics*, ed. P. Benacerraf and H. Putnam, pp. 274–289.

Beth, E. W. *The Foundations of Mathematics*. Amsterdam: North Holland Publishing Company, 1969.

Black, Max. "The Elusiveness of Sets." *Review of Metaphysics*, 24 (1971), 614–636.

———. *Margins of Precision*. Ithaca, N.Y.: Cornell University Press, 1972.

Brentano, Franz. *The True and the Evident*, ed. Oskar Kraus, trans. Roderick M. Chisholm. New York: Humanities Press, 1966.

Brouwer, L. E. J. "Consciousness, Philosophy and Mathematics." *Library of the Tenth International Congress of Philosophy*, vol. 1. Amsterdam, 1948, pp. 1235–1249.

———. "Historical Background, Principles and Methods of Intuitionism." *South African Journal of Science*, 49 (1952), 139–146.

———. "On the Significance of the Principle of the Excluded Third in Mathematics." In *From Frege to Gödel*, ed. J. van Heijenoort, pp. 335–345.

———. "Points and Spaces." *Canadian Journal of Mathematics*, 6 (1945), 1–17.

Carnap, Rudolf. "Empiricism, Semantics, and Ontology." In *Philosophy of Mathematics*, ed. P. Benacerraf and H. Putnam, pp. 233–249.

Carr, D., and E. S. Casey, eds. *Explorations in Phenomenology*. The Hague: Martinus Nijhoff, 1973.

Cartwright, Richard. "Propositions." In *Analytic Philosophy, First Series*, ed. R. Butler. Oxford: Blackwell, 1956, pp. 81–103.

Chang, C. C., and H. J. Keisler. *Continuous Model Theory*. Annals of Mathematical Studies, no. 58. Princeton, N.J.: Princeton University Press, 1966.

Chihara, Charles S. *Ontology and the Vicious Circle Principle*. Ithaca, N.Y.: Cornell University Press, 1973.

Church, Alonzo. "The Need for Abstract Entities in Semantics." In *The Structure of Language*, ed. J. W. Fodor and J. J. Katz, pp. 437–446.

Cohen, Paul J. *Set Theory and the Continuum Hypothesis*. Menlo Park, Calif.: Benjamin, 1966.

Dauben, J. W. "The Trigometric Background to Georg Cantor's Theory of Sets." *Archive for the History of Exact Science*, 7 (1971), 181–216.

Dedekind, Richard. "Continuity and Irrational Numbers." In Richard Dedekind, *Theory of Numbers*. New York: Dover Publications, 1963.

Dreyfus, Hubert. "The Perceptual Noema: Gurwitsch's Crucial Contribution." In *Life-World and Consciousness: Essays for Aron Gurwitsch*, ed. L. E. Embree. Evanston, Ill.: Northwestern University Press, 1972, pp. 135–171.

Euclid. *Euclid's Elements*. Vol. 2, ed. and trans. T. L. Heath. New York: Dover Publications, 1956.

Feyerabend, Paul K. "Explanation, Reduction, and Empiricism." In *Minnesota Studies in the Philosophy of Science*, vol. 3, ed. Herbert Feigl and Grover Maxwell. Minneapolis: University of Minnesota Press, 1962.

Figueiredo, Djairo Guedes de. "Decompositions of the Sphere." *Notas de Mathematica* no. 14. Rio de Janeiro, 1958.

Fine, Arthur. "How to Compare Theories: Reference and Change." *Nous*, 9 (1975), 17–32.

Fodor, J. A., and J. J. Katz, eds. *The Structure of Language*. Englewood Cliffs, N.J.: Prentice-Hall, 1964.

Føllesdal, Dagfinn. "Husserl's Notion of Noema." *Journal of Philosophy*, 66 (1969), 680–687.

———. "Phenomenology for Analytic Philosophers." In *Philosophy in Scandinavia*, ed. R. Olsen and A. Paul. Baltimore: The Johns Hopkins Press, 1972.

Frege, G. "On Sense and Reference." In *Translations from the Writings of Gottlob Frege,* ed. P. Geach and Max Black. Oxford: Blackwell, 1960), pp. 56–78.

———. "The Thought." In *Philosophical Logic,* ed. P. F. Strawson.

Friedländer, Paul. *Plato.* New York: Harper and Row, 1958.

Gödel, Kurt. "What Is Cantor's Continuum Problem?" In *Philosophy of Mathematics,* ed. P. Benacerraf and H. Putnam, pp. 258–274.

Grandy, Richard. "Some Remarks about Logical Form." *Nous,* 8 (1974), 157–164.

Grzegorczyk, A. "A Philosophically Plausible Formal Interpretation of Intuitionistic Logic." *Indagationes Mathematicae,* 26 (1964), 596–601. Press, 1969.

Hanson, N. R. *Patterns of Discovery.* Cambridge: Cambridge University Press, 1969.

Hardy, G. H. *A Course of Pure Mathematics.* 10th ed. Cambridge: Cambridge University Press, 1958.

Heijenoort, J. van, ed. *From Frege to Gödel: A Source Book in Mathematical Logic, 1879–1931.* Cambridge, Mass.: Harvard University Press, 1967.

Hempel, Carl. *Aspects of Scientific Explanation.* New York: Free Press, 1965.

———. "Empiricist Criteria of Cognitive Significance." In Carl Hempel, *Aspects of Scientific Explanation,* pp. 102–107.

Heyting, Arend. *Intuitionism.* Amsterdam: North Holland Publishing Company, 1956.

Hurewicz, W., and H. Wallman. *Dimension Theory.* Princeton, N.J.: Princeton University Press, 1948.

Husserl, Edmund. *Cartesian Meditations,* trans. D. Cairns. The Hague: Martinus Nijhoff, 1960.

———. *The Crisis of the European Sciences and Transcendental Phenomenology,* trans. D. Carr. Evanston, Ill.: Northwestern University Press, 1970.

———. *Formal and Transcendental Logic,* trans. D. Cairns. The Hague: Martinus Nijhoff, 1969.

———. *The Idea of Phenomenology,* trans. W. P. Alston and G. Nakhnikian. The Hague: Martinus Nijhoff, 1964.

———. *Ideas,* trans. W. R. B. Gibson. New York: Humanities Press, 1969.

———. *Logical Investigations,* trans. J. N. Findlay. New York: Humanities Press, 1970.

Jacob, François. *The Logic of Life,* trans. B. E. Spillmann. New York: Pantheon, 1973.

Kleene, S. C. *Introduction to Metamathematics*. New York: Van Nostrand, 1962.

——, and R. E. Vesley. *The Foundations of Intuitionistic Mathematics*. Amsterdam: North Holland Publishing Company, 1965.

Manheim, J. H. *The Genesis of Point Set Topology*. London: Pergamon Press, 1964.

Myhill, John. "Empirical Meaningfulness and Intuitionistic Logic." *Philosophy and Phenomenological Research*, 33 (1972), 186–191.

Parsons, Charles. "Comments." In *From Frege to Gödel*, ed. J. van Heijenoort, pp. 447–453.

——. "Ontology and Mathematics." *Philosophical Review*, 80 (1972), 151–176.

——. "A Plea for Substitutional Quantification Theory." *Journal of Philosophy*, 68 (1971), 231–238.

Parsons, Kathryn Pyne. "On Criteria of Meaning Change." *British Journal of Philosophy of Science*, 22 (1971), 131–144.

Peirce, Charles. "Critical Review of Berkeley's Idealism." In *Values in a Universe of Chance*, ed. P. P. Wiener. Garden City, N.Y.: Doubleday, 1958, pp. 73–91.

Polya, G. *How To Solve It*. Princeton, N.J.: Princeton University Press, 1945.

Prawitz, Dag. "Constructive Semantics." In *Proceedings of the First Scandinavian Logic Symposium*. Uppsala, 1970, pp. 96–114.

——. *Natural Deduction: A Proof-Theoretical Study*. Stockholm: Almquist and Wiksell, 1965.

Quine, W. V. O. "Existence and Quantification." In W. V. O. Quine, *Ontological Relativity*, pp. 91–114.

——. *From a Logical Point of View*. Cambridge, Mass.: Harvard University Press, 1961.

——. *Methods of Logic*. Rev. ed. New York: Holt, Rinehart and Winston, 1961.

——. *Ontological Relativity and Other Essays*. New York: Columbia University Press, 1969.

——. *Philosophy of Logic*. Englewood Cliffs, N.J.: Prentice-Hall, 1970.

——. "Truth by Convention." In *Philosophy of Mathematics*, ed. P. Benacerraf and H. Putnam, pp. 322–346.

——. *Word and Object*. New York: John Wiley and Sons, 1960.

Reid, Constance. *Hilbert*. New York: Springer-Verlag, 1972.

Rota, Gian-Carlo. "Edmund Husserl and the Reform of Logic." In *Explorations in Phenomenology*, ed. D. Carr and E. S. Casey, pp. 299–305.

Scheffler, Israel. *Science and Subjectivity.* New York: Bobbs-Merrill, 1967.

Smith, D. W., and R. MacIntyre. "Husserl's Identification of Meaning and Noema." *The Monist,* 59 (1975), 115–133.

——. "Intentionality via Intensions." *Journal of Philosophy,* 68 (1971), 541–561.

Smorynski, C. Review of Bowen's "An Extension of the Intuitionistic Propositional Calculus." *Mathematical Reviews,* 45 (1973), no. 3161.

Stenius, Erik. "Sets." *Synthese,* 27 (1974), 161–188.

Strawson, P. F., ed. *Philosophical Logic.* Oxford: Oxford University Press, 1968.

Tarski, Alfred. "The Concept of Truth in Formalized Languages." In Tarski, *Logic, Semantics, and Metamathematics,* pp. 152–279.

——. *Logic, Semantics, and Metamathematics.* Trans. J. H. Woodger. Oxford: Oxford University Press, 1956.

Thomson, J. F. "Truth-Bearers and the Trouble about Propositions." *Journal of Philosophy,* 66 (1969), 737–747.

Tragesser, Robert. "Eidetic Analysis, Informal Rigor, and a Phenomenological Critique of Carnap's Notion of Explication." *Philosophy and Phenomenological Research,* 33 (1972), 48–61.

——. "On the Phenomenological Foundations of Mathematics." In *Explorations in Phenomenology,* ed. D. Carr and E. S. Casey, pp. 285–298.

——. "Some Observations Concerning Logic and Concepts of Existence." *Journal of Philosophy,* 69 (1972), 375–383.

Wallace, John. "Convention T and Substitutional Quantification." *Nous,* 5 (1971), 199–211.

Wang, H. "Certain Predicates Defined by Induction Schemata." *Journal of Symbolic Logic,* 18 (1953), 49–59.

Weyl, Hermann. *Das Kontinuum.* New York: Chelsea Publishing Company, n.d.

——. *Philosophy of Mathematics and Natural Science.* New York: Atheneum, 1963.

——. *Symmetry.* Princeton, N.J.: Princeton University Press, 1952.

Zucker, Jeffrey. "The Adequacy Problem for Inferential Logic." University of Utrecht Mathematics Preprints, Preprint Number 37, November 1976.

——. "The Adequacy Problem for Classical Logic." University of Utrecht Mathematics Preprints, forthcoming.

| Index

Phenomenology and Logic

Designed by R. E. Rosenbaum.
Composed by Vail-Ballou Press, Inc.
in 11 point linotype Baskerville, 2 points leaded,
with display lines in monotype Baskerville.
Printed letterpress from type by Vail-Ballou
on Warren's Number 66 text, 50 pound basis.
Bound by Vail-Ballou
in Joanna book cloth
and stamped in All Purpose foil.

Library of Congress Cataloging in Publication Data
(For library cataloging purposes only)

Tragesser, Robert S. 1943–
  Phenomenology and logic.

  Bibliography: p.
  Includes index.
  1. Phenomenology. 2. Logic. 3. Husserl, Edmund, 1859–1938. I. Title.
B829.5.T66   142.'7   76-28025
ISBN 0-8014-1068-1